How to Buy a Single-Engine Airplane

HOW TO BUY A SINGLE-ENGINE AIRPLANE

SCOTT "SKY" SMITH

MBI Publishing Company

First published in 2001 by MBI Publishing Company, Galtier Plaza, Suite 200, 380 Jackson Street, St. Paul, MN 55101-3885 USA

Library of Congress Cataloging-in-Publication Data Available

ISBN 0-7603-1008-4

On the front cover: Built from 1961 to 1975, the Piper Cherokee 180 was one of the first true, four-place, single-engine aircraft. Not to mention the fact that it combines good performance and simplicity. Finally, pilots could fill their seats with people and still have room for fuel. *Photo courtesy of Norm Goyer*

On the back cover. Left: The Cessna 172 Skyhawk is perhaps the quintessential single-engine aircraft. Thousands were built from 1956 through 1986, first with a six-cylinder Continental engine, then with a four-cylinder Lycoming. Cessna resumed production of the 172 in 1997. *Photo courtesy of Cessna Aircraft Company* ***Right:*** The 1999 Piper Archer III is loaded with avionics, including a stormscope and three-axis autopilot. Piper has cranked out a good number of Archers since beginning production in 1976. *Photo courtesy of Norm Goyer*

Edited by Dennis Pernu

Printed in the United States of America

Contents

Chapter 1

Selecting the Aircraft That's Right for You

Buying an aircraft is a major decision. Not just because an aircraft costs money (so do cars, boats, and computers), but also because an aircraft purchase puts a lot of things at risk. Considerations like personal safety and financial security can be compromised. Sometimes an aircraft does more than the buyer needs, costs more than the buyer can afford, or is more difficult to operate than the buyer expected. Each problem by itself can be manageable, but put two together and the aircraft can sit idle in the hangar or even become a dangerous weapon. Buyers try and make buying an aircraft a practical or rational decision, but in reality it's mostly emotional. If you have done the research for the purchase and have made the decision to move from renter to owner, the only decision left is what aircraft you want to own and fly.

The Pitts Special S1S and aircraft like it are desired by many ego personalities.

Because we buy an aircraft to fly it, an aircraft that doesn't get in the air (due to finances, pilot skill, etc.) isn't a good purchase.

Making the decision to buy an aircraft is really the easy part. Deciding what kind of aircraft to buy takes a lot of time and research. Many aircraft buyers end up making their purchase decisions based on what they want, not what they need or will use. Remember that the purchase of an aircraft is largely emotional. Buying on emotion requires us to look at our "inner pilot" and evaluate our needs as well as our personality. The right aircraft needs to satisfy both the owner's emotional and practical requirements. An owner should be comfortable (not complacent or careless, but *comfortable*) when flying in all conditions. No matter how nice an aircraft is, if the owner dislikes its looks, its color, or the way it handles in a crosswind, it will sit abandoned in the hangar, awaiting a new owner who will appreciate its capabilities while the old owner complains about what a "bad" aircraft it is.

Personalities

If you're involved in aviation, there must be a little bit of ego deep down inside your "inner pilot." "Ego," according to *Webster's Dictionary*, means, in part, "self-esteem" and "self-respect" to "distinguish yourself from others." And aviation and aircraft ownership *do* require self-esteem and self-respect—a special someone who wants the freedom and control that flying an aircraft provides. Aviation also brings out a feeling of accomplishment and admiration that many people desire. Having a little bit of ego doesn't mean that we want to be in the spotlight all the time. What it *does* mean is that we like the idea of taking a different path in our life: a path that others decided was too difficult or too costly to undertake. Pilots look for recognition from those non-pilots in their circle of contacts. It *does* take dedication and a strong personality to obtain any license in aviation, and a private pilot is rightly as proud as any airline pilot, for he or she has obtained a status that many people only dream about.

Robert Armstrong is a great example of a world-class aerobatic competition pilot who relies on skill and a professional attitude.

So What Is Your Personality?

It's already established that you have a little bit of ego or you wouldn't be a pilot, but what's the overwhelming trait that will influence how you will use an aircraft and what aircraft will make you happy? Let's start with the "egotistical" personality. Typically in aviation this trait leads to overconfidence and the need for attention. Someone looking for an aircraft that exhibits pizzazz, unique looks, or a specific style typifies this personality. The egotistical pilot looks for an aircraft that exudes excitement to the people who see it. What would that person buy? Possibly a Pitts Special biplane, or maybe a Wilga or Socata Tobago. Or perhaps they'd like a Mooney. Oftentimes these owners like custom-built aircraft or sporty (looking and flying) factory-builts. Looks and performance are the key. It's not unusual for these owners to drive ground-based vehicles that represent their egos. You just might see them drive to the local airport in their excitement-oozing, high-performance Corvette convertible or Jaguar XJS.

The Cessna 210 is preferred by the "dominate/driver" personality.

Other pilots fall into the "dominate/driver" personality. Often they are upper-level managers, self-employed, or business owners. They like to control their flying just like they control their everyday activities. They set the time they fly and the places they travel to. Weather and distance are not factors, or at least not major factors that stop them from planned trips. The aircraft that dominate/driver personalities fly need to meet and maintain the schedules they set. They typically need all-weather aircraft and the pilot skills to fly those aircraft. Dominate/driver pilots like aircraft like the Beechcraft Bonanza A36, the Cessna 210 and light and medium twin-engine aircraft like the Cessna 310, Piper Seneca, and Beechcraft Baron. But don't be surprised to see these owners flying cabin-class singles and twins like Malibus, Cessna 400 Series aircraft, or Piper Navajo variations.

These aircraft satisfy the requirements of all-weather and long-range flying. That often means they're pressurized and have de-icing equipment. It might also mean they're turbine powered! Aircraft like the TBM 700 or the Pilatus are two owner-flown turbine singles that could fill the needs of these pilots. Custom-built aircraft of this ilk include the Lancair and Glasair aircraft lines, as well as the new wave of custom-built turbojet aircraft like the Maverick, Eclipse, Vantage, and Sapphire. When dominate/driver pilots show up at the hangar, they'll probably be in large sedans or sport utility vehicles made by Mercedes, Cadillac, Lexus, and BMW.

What if you're not a demanding type? Maybe you're more interested in safety than looks (not that pilots are looking for unsafe aircraft); your personality might be more of the "stable" type. Also known as "complacent" (while not the best name for a pilot), the stable personality looks for safety, ease of flying, and comfort, not speed and looks. Stable pilots' egos might "want" flashy or high-performance aircraft, but the inner pilots in them keep them looking and

A "stable" pilot looks for safety, comfort, and practicality to meet his or her everyday needs.

The custom-built KR2 is an example of an economical and efficient aircraft. An analytical personality looks for the most for the money: the most speed for the lowest cost.

flying basic, all-around aircraft. Usually they own and fly Cessna 172s or 182s, Piper Cherokees, and many of the custom canard variants (Velocity, Long Eze, etc.) that promote safety and simplicity of flying. While fixed gears and fixed propellers are not requirements, these simple aircraft traits dominate the aircraft a stable pilot would own and fly.

This is a large segment of the aviation population. When you ride to the airport with a stable pilot you'll probably ride in a sport utility vehicle manufactured by Ford, Chevy, or Dodge—or even in a station wagon.

Are you one of those pilots who likes the finer points of an aircraft? Are you looking for the most efficient aircraft on the market? If so, you may be an analytical person. "Analytical" pilots look at the details, the numbers. They like efficiency, low drag coefficients, and low operation costs, but not at the expense of high performance. Analytical pilots look for the most for the money when buying an aircraft or a car.

The analytical pilot will also surprise some people. They might fly a Mooney because of the performance versus the cost to operate. Or, they'll fly a Cessna 150 because of its overall low cost to own. Analytical pilots also like the custom-built aircraft market because they feel these aircraft have so much more to offer in speed, fuel efficiency, and performance. Plus, they can build the aircraft and make sure that each detail meets their particular analytical needs. They'll also surprise you at the local car dealer. They could be picking out a Volvo or Saab just as easily as they'd buy an extended-cab pickup or Volkswagen Beetle.

Abilities

There's more to selecting and owning an aircraft than just personalities. Your pilot abilities, skill level, age, certificates, and ratings are also important in the preliminary decision-making process. If you are a student or a private pilot, it's probably in your best interest to start with the smaller, less complicated aircraft. And as your skill increases and you add advanced ratings to your pilot's license, you can change the aircraft you fly. But when starting out, it's best to stay with the simple and basic aircraft.

The aviation industry actually promotes the gradual or "step up" process in aircraft ownership. Manufacturers usually build trainers as two- or four-seat aircraft that are extremely simple to learn to fly. Even the certificate and rating processes are designed in steps. For example, first is dual instruction, then solo flight, and then the license. And the licenses are in steps: recreational first, followed by private, instrument, commercial, multi-engine, airline transport, and so on.

Before you move into a twin, the FAA and insurance underwriters will expect you to gradually move up the airplane ladder without skipping steps.

Training can be critically important and affect your insurance premiums and claims.

Advanced ratings, like advanced aircraft, require completion of time and/or experience at a certain level before you make the next step.

Aircraft ownership is the same. Sure, you can skip the steps just as you can with advanced ratings. A multi-engine rating is available before the instrument rating or the commercial certificate. And the ownership of a heavy single or twin is possible before the private license is obtained. Practical? Probably not. But it is possible. What keeps most people from taking those big steps and skipping the lower levels of ownership? Personality, cost to operate, and often insurance. The aviation insurance industry is probably the biggest hurdle in moving up the aircraft ladder too fast. If you do have the rating but not the experience, the insurance underwriter will probably *not* provide the coverage and vice versa: just because you have experience doesn't automatically guarantee insurance coverage. And if the insurance company *does* provide coverage, it might be financially prohibitive.

The ability to obtain training can also have a significant impact on the type of aircraft you buy. If the location where you will be keeping the aircraft doesn't offer training for the type of aircraft you want,

Just because you like an aircraft and it does what you want it to do doesn't mean you will be able to get the required training. Finding an instructor who has adequate hours to meet your insurance guidelines may be impossible in your location. You may need to get factory training or factory-approved training, find an instructor within a reasonable (or unreasonable) distance, or be prepared to fly without insurance as you accumulate the hours necessary to obtain it. *Photo courtesy of Cessna Aircraft Company*

maybe you'll need a different aircraft (or a new location). Conventional or tailwheel aircraft and custom-built aircraft are probably the biggest problem. Qualified tailwheel instructors have become harder and harder to locate. Most new instructors have gotten their training in tri-gear aircraft, which has become the standard in certified aircraft. tailwheel aircraft are still available on the used market and in limited quantities as new or custom-built aircraft. But sales history has shown that tri-gear aircraft are the most popular and used most often as trainers. Additionally, tailwheel aircraft require more attention and proficiency than do their tri-gear cousins. But this doesn't mean you don't have to stay proficient in a tri-gear.

This problem isn't reserved for tailwheel pilots. Training can also be difficult to find if you own a unique or low-production aircraft. Flight instructors with experience in an aircraft that's very old or unique can be hard to find, thus making training a major cost or a complicated process. A good example are Grumman aircraft, which use castering nose wheels and differential braking: not many instructors have experience in this kind of aircraft. In addition most insurance companies won't allow instruction by an inexperienced flight instructor in these aircraft. While most aircraft won't be a problem, you'll have to be careful with a few individual models.

Owning an aircraft, like anything else, requires money, whether it's paying for the fuel, the hangar, the annual, or even your visual flight rules (VFR) charts. If you can't pay the expenses associated with owning the aircraft, you probably won't fly the aircraft. And as owners we want to fly! Therefore, it's important that the aircraft you decide to buy is one that you have the ability to pay for. Many an owner has bought an aircraft and has been unable to afford the regular monthly costs. Travel the local airports and see how many aircraft sit for unusual amounts of time. Often the owner bought more than he or she could afford. Pride and embarrassment won't allow them to sell the aircraft and buy something that's really in their price range.

Prior to the purchase, the buyer should develop a payment plan that includes money set-aside to replace or repair the "time between overhaul" (TBO) or time-life items on the aircraft (the engine and propeller, to name a couple). A system should also be established to accommodate any unscheduled repairs needed during the ownership. Usually, funds set-aside for repairs or maintenance should be calculated on an hourly basis. This is where owner or owner-assisted maintenance can help keep the ownership costs down. Many things that the owner can do are described in the Federal Aviation Administration's (FAA) Federal Aviation Regulations (FAR). FAR Part 43 addresses the specific items that qualified owners who are not licensed FAA maintenance personnel can complete. Every owner needs to review and be familiar with those items.

Use of the Aircraft

Another "before you buy" step is to think about how you fly. What do you plan on doing with your aircraft? Do you plan to travel long distances? And will you be traveling long distances on every flight? How many people usually ride with you? What would you like to do with your aircraft? Aerobatics? Racing? Sightseeing? Unfortunately, there is not one aircraft that can do everything, but there are a lot of aircraft that can do a lot of different things. Picking the best one for you means deciding what's most important.

The aircraft you buy should meet the majority of your needs the majority of the time. If you fly locally or under a 300-mile radius of home, buy an aircraft that works well for that. Many pleasure flights are made with one or two people on board. If that's the case in your

This Smith MiniPlane is highly modified with an engine that produces twice the power and a wing span that is 4 feet shorter than the original 17-foot design. Its sole purpose was to compete at the Reno Air Races.

The Extra was originally designed for aerobatics but has evolved into a limited, all-purpose aircraft, providing reasonable cross-country capabilities and aerobatics.

flying career, why buy an aircraft that has a number of empty seats every time you go for a flight? You can always rent an aircraft for those occasional cross-country trips or the time you need to take an extra couple of friends with you. Many a buyer has bought an aircraft for the occasional application and not been able to fly it for the regular uses. These are the owners who have an aircraft in a hangar and ride with you to the local fly-in. Additionally, the cost of operating some of the larger and more complex aircraft restricts some owners from using them on a regular basis. They fly the occasional long trip but decide not to fly the short hops because they usually cost too much.

Location of the Aircraft

Where you keep your aircraft will affect how often you fly it: not a profound statement, just common sense. The further your plane is from home, the less you'll

If you want to spend your time on the water, you will need to find a sea base where you can keep your float-equipped airplane, perhaps a Piper Super Cub.

fly! The most desirable location to base your aircraft would be in your backyard. That means we should all live in an airpark with our hangar and home attached. But, if that's not a possibility, the next best thing is to have your aircraft at an airport within 30 minutes of home. We know that in some areas, that's just not possible. In those instances, it's just best to try and locate and use an airport that is as close as possible. Obviously, having to spend hours in the car driving to the airport to fly will greatly diminish the hours you spend flying.

The type of runway surface and length will also be a factor in the type of aircraft owned. High-performance or retractable-gear aircraft typically require a hard-surface and fairly long runway. Grass, gravel, and dirt are better suited to fixed-gear and tailwheel aircraft. And insurance companies feel the same way. They might not provide coverage for a retractable on grass.

The location you choose needs to provide not only training, as mentioned earlier, but also maintenance services for your aircraft type. Tube-and-fabric construction needs a mechanic that can repair a tube-and-fabric aircraft. If one is not available at your airport, you'll have to move your aircraft somewhere else, and that costs time and money. If your aircraft is a non-electric aircraft without permanent radios and a transponder, you probably won't want to base it at an airport that requires constant communication—and they probably won't want you there either.

Another concern is the availability of hangar space at the airport of your choice. If you buy a fabric or composite aircraft, it really needs to be in a hangar. If you have a metal aircraft, you could get by with storing it on the ramp. But even with a metal aircraft, storage in the elements reduces the life (and possibly the value) of exterior, interior, windows, and windshields. It's highly recommended that if you don't have the option of a fully enclosed hangar, you'll probably want a cockpit cover (or at least a windshield cover). Any extra protection from the elements can extend the life of the paint, interior, and avionics. And it's important to not only protect from the wrath of Mother Nature, but also to deter potential unscrupulous behavior at the airport (i.e., vandalism and theft).

Cost Analysis of an Aircraft

Money and the cost of operation weigh heavily and can greatly influence the final purchase decision. So

Sometimes the best airplane for your money and needs comes in a box, like this PL200RG kit.

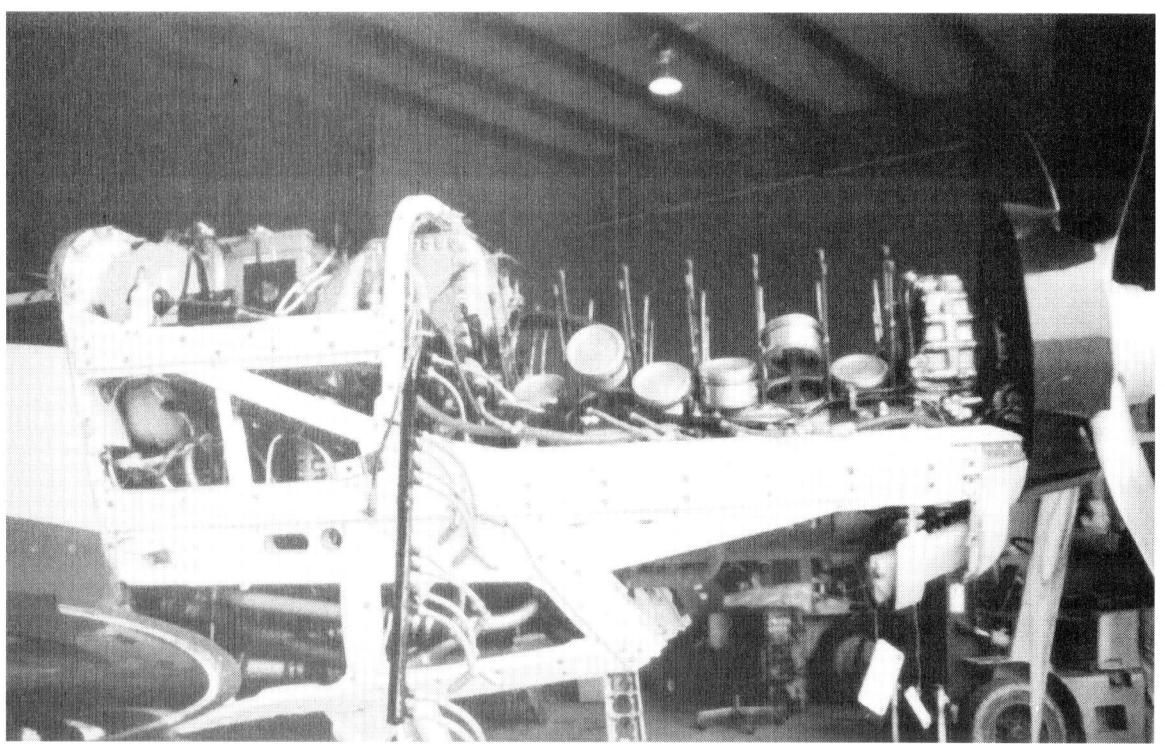

Catastrophic failures and unexpected repairs greatly increase the cost of airplane ownership.

prior to making your final choice, figure out your dream aircraft's hourly operational cost. The rule of thumb is to estimate the cost of the fuel burn for the aircraft and then use a multiplier. In the single-engine case, for example, the cost of fuel per hour times two should yield the basic operational cost for the aircraft. This does not include items like insurance, hangar, and training, but it should be a good estimate for the operation of the aircraft.

For a complete annual operational cost analysis you will need to first consider and estimate your total number of flying hours per year. The figure that most owners use for ownership calculations is 100 hours a year. When figuring the cost of ownership you should also consider the following: fuel and oil usage; annual inspections; unscheduled maintenance and airworthiness directives (ADs); oil and filter changes; insurance premiums; principal and interest; engine set-aside; hangars or tie downs; license requirements like biannual flight reviews and physicals; Global Positioning System (GPS), sectional, and chart

Aircraft Hourly Operational Cost Rule of Thumb

The hourly operating cost of a light, single-engine aircraft (not including principle interest, hangar, or insurance) is three times the cost of fuel per hour.

Example: $3 per gallon x 10 GPH = $30
$30 x 2 = $60 per hour to operate

The hourly operating cost of a heavy, single-engine aircraft is three times the fuel cost per hour.

Example: $3 per gallon x 15 GPH = $45
$45 x 2.5 = $112.50 per hour to operate

The hourly operating cost of a light, twin-engine aircraft is four times the fuel cost per hour.

Example: $3 per gallon x 25 GPH = $75
$75 x 3 = $225 per hour to operate

Date________________ AIRCRAFT INSURANCE QUOTE REQUEST

SkySmith International, LTD.
dba SkySmith International Insurance Agency Inc.
2525 NW 71st Place, Ankeny, IA 50021-9048

Voice: 515-289-1439 *800-743-1439
Fax: 773-326-0690
E-Mail: www.skysmith.com or ins@skysmith.com

For your no obligation aviation insurance quote, please complete the following and return. If you have any questions or need immediate service, please call or fax to the above numbers. (some restrictions may apply)

*=prefers

Individual or Partnership or Corporation or LLC Holding Co.
Name____
Address____
Address____
City, State, Zip____

Home #________________________________
Work #________________________________
Fax#________________________________
Cell #________________________________
E-Mail________________________________

Please complete this form and attach an additional sheet of paper for explanations if necessary.

Year:_______; Aircraft:_________; FAA N#:________; Seats:________; Gear Type: Tri, RG, TW ; Engine: Fixed 2- 1-_____

Airworthiness Certificate: **Std or Exp or Othe**r; Is Certificate in full force & effect? Circle **YES** or **NO**

Storage: **Hangared or Tied Out or Other**:_______________; Airport, State:__________________,____; ID:_______

Runway: **Paved or Grass or Other**:_________________; Length:___________; Modifications? Circle **YES** or **NO**

Aircraft Use: **Pleasure and/or Business or Commercial:**____;

Lienholder:____; Amount of Lien:_______________; BOW: **YES** or **NO**

Additional Insured:____;

Coverages: Builder's Risk or Liab Only or GNIM or G&T (GNIF) or G&F; Deductables: $_____NIM/$____In Motion;

Hull Coverage:$___________; Liability:$1,000,000 _________per occurrence; Limited to $100,000 _____per passenger;

Medical:$________ per passenger; Extra Coverages? Non-Owned, Premise, IAC Competition, Foreign Travel, _______;

Named Pilots-- REQUIRED for EACH PILOT who will OPERATE THE AIRCRAFT (Total time / and last 12 months total time) ***Dates of***
Name Age/B Date Occupation Certificates & Ratings Total Time/ Last 12 mos. This Aircraft Tailwheel Retract Multi ***Medical & BFR***

#1____

#2____

#3____

#4____

For the above Named Pilots, please answer the following questions and explain any "yes" answers on an additional sheet of paper:

Accidents, Violations, Waivers or Auto Convictions (other than speeding tickets): **Y or N** ; if yes, explain ____________________

Current Insurance Company ________________ (New Purchase) Effective Date ____________(ASAP) Exp Premium $____________

Comments: ____

Source ____________________

updates; recurrent training costs; and instrument flight rules (IFR) currency.

Let's set up an example using a four-place, fixed-gear, fixed-propeller aircraft with a retail purchase price of $40,000. We'll have an estimated fuel burn of 8 gallons per hour and oil consumption of about 14 quarts per year (or about 1 quart every seven hours).

The annual inspection will be about $500. As the name implies, this is for an inspection only. The basic annual inspection does not include any labor or the cost of use in any repairs, even though most owners expect them to. Additionally, unexpected repairs are always possible, so the owner should set-aside money to fix these small "surprises."

Usually, if you set-aside a percentage of the value, in this case 6 percent was used, for unscheduled maintenance, you should be able to fix the minor breakdowns or glitches that show up during the year. If the aircraft is older (more than 30 years) you should probably increase the percentage to compensate for the age. If the aircraft is 10 years old or less (maybe up to 15 years, depending on its maintenance), you might be able to lower the percentage. Yet another variable in this part of the calculation is if the aircraft is complex. The more complicated the aircraft (i.e., more moving parts), the higher the percentage that should be set-aside for unexpected repairs.

Fixing minor problems is part of a preventative maintenance program that seems to prolong the life of

Complete Annual Operational Cost Analysis Worksheet

Fuel Burn
(Gallons per hour x cost per gallon x hours flown per year) __________

Oil Used
(Cost per quart x quarts used per year) __________

Annual Inspection
(Base rate for aircraft in your area) __________

Unscheduled Maintenance
(6% [for 10-year-old aircraft] x aircraft purchase price) __________

Oil Changes
(Cost per oil change x number of changes per year) __________

Insurance Premium
(Average is about 3% x cost of aircraft) __________

Interest Costs
(Current interest rate x purchase price of aircraft) __________

Engine Set-Aside
(Cost of engine / hours before TBO x hours flown per year) __________

Hangar or Tie-Down
(Cost per year) __________

Biennial Flight Review and Flight Physical
(Cost per year) __________

Information Updates
(Cost per year) __________

Total Annual Cost to Operate
(Total above figures) __________

Estimated Hourly Cost to Operate
(Total annual cost / hours flown per year) __________

an aircraft. Most mechanics will tell you that oil changes are a necessity for good preventative maintenance, not an option. So, if we plan on four oil changes a year at 25-hour intervals, we would have a total of about $400.

Aviation insurance is another major variable. Typically, a low-time private pilot in this type of aircraft will pay premiums of less than $100 per month. Rates and underwriting requirements change constantly, so this is a factor that has to be recalculated on every policy renewal date. If you borrow money—or if you want to consider that your money has an investment value—you need to calculate the interest that you would pay or possibly lose while paying off the aircraft. Using just simple interest calculations and an average current interest rate (currently 12 percent), we would have to aside about $4,800 a year.

One of the most important parts of the aircraft (and the most expensive) is the engine. In a small four-place aircraft, the engine would cost about $15,000 to replace. That means that we need to set-aside about $7.50 an hour if it's a brand-new, zero-time engine. If it has say, 1,000 hours left before the recommended overhaul time, we'd set-aside $15 per hour based on 100 hours a year.

Also included in this complete cost analysis is a hangar rental fee of $150 per month. (At home, I could tie down for free, but my insurance would be higher. This is another huge variable.) Finally, plan on spending about $100-plus per year for your biannual flight review and flight physicals, and $200-plus for information updates. Recurrent training is minimal for this type of aircraft and IFR currency is not necessarily required.

These basic numbers would also work for a two-place, custom-built aircraft. Many people believe that they can buy a completed custom-built aircraft and save money. But don't plan on the savings you'll get from buying and flying an already-completed custom-built aircraft instead of a factory-built aircraft just yet. Wait until you get those numbers and calculate them separately. Note that this example didn't consider any principal or any opportunity for investment gains or losses. Also missing are calculations for depreciation.

Building and maintaining your own airplane can help cut the costs of ownership significantly.

The point is to understand the process and fill in the numbers appropriate for you, your location, and your dream aircraft.

One thing that you must always remember about pilots is that they have their own way of looking at things. "Just a different perspective," is what most pilots would say. If you use "pilot math," for example, the more hours you fly the cheaper the cost per hour. If you fly 200 hours annually rather than 100, the hourly cost will be cut in half, right? Remember, the inverse may also be true: even if you don't fly 100 hours per year there is still a significant amount of fixed costs that don't change with the number of hours you fly.

An extreme example is an owner whose aircraft went through a total restoration worth about $75,000 in one year. During that year of restoration the owner only got to fly the aircraft about one hour. That calculates to about $75,000 per hour! Compare that to the cost of a rental at the local airport. Another sobering fact is that a $20,000 plane's operational cost per hour will not be 50 percent of the $40,000 example given earlier. Certain fixed costs don't change.

Buyers need to fine-tune estimated hourly operational costs. These hourly costs can vary substantially depending on each unique situation. A student pilot's insurance, for example, can be 35 percent or more higher than a private pilot's. Commercial and instrument ratings can decrease the annual premium. People located at high-demand airports may pay up to $1,000 per month to rent a hangar. Fuel, oil, and labor vary by airport and state. Interest varies depending on term, collateral, and amount financed.

Neither repairs resulting from the annual nor catastrophic costs are included because they can vary dramatically. To establish the engine set-aside, the hours remaining on the engine are critical; the fewer hours that are left, the more money per hour that needs to be set-aside. The cost of your annual partially depends on what you have done during the year, or the unscheduled maintenance. Inadequate oil and filter changes or lack of regular use may shorten your engine's life.

About now, many of you are thinking about that custom-built plane. Seems like the way to cut operational costs. But remember, if you buy someone else's custom-built aircraft, a mechanic is required to do the maintenance. (The builder is the manufacturer, comparable to a factory such as Cessna or Piper.) Many states and local FAA Flight Standards District Offices (FSDOs) will allow the owner to do a lot of the maintenance, just like on a certified factory aircraft. But the buyer still needs to figure the real cost into the expense.

Ownership Options

There are options other than buying an aircraft. Many owners have found happiness in partnerships, flying clubs, and just renting aircraft. Most of us have the desire to be the sole owner of our "dream" aircraft. But sometimes that's just not possible. Partnerships are the next step. Find the right partner, share the costs, and enjoy a great aircraft. Partnerships can also allow you to purchase more aircraft than you might be able to afford as a single owner. The "fantasy" partner is probably a silent partner that paid for half the aircraft and shares half the bills but hates to, or never wants to, fly. Partnerships can be very satisfactory in some situations.

Another ownership option is a corporate job that allows you to fly the company aircraft. Wouldn't it be great to have an employer that always sends you where you want to go? Many people have always admired military pilots because they get to fly all the neat stuff while the taxpayers pay for the fuel and maintenance. Some people have all the fun without any of the expense! But for those of us that have to buy our own fuel and pay our own maintenance bills, keeping the costs down are extremely important.

Still another cost-cutting ownership option is to build your own aircraft and be your own mechanic. More custom aircraft kits and aircraft are being sold, built, and flown annually than factory planes. But even a custom-built aircraft can be expensive to own. Custom-built aircraft require a commitment of not only money, but also a large amount of time. And they are not built on an assembly line with years of production history. A factory aircraft has thousands of hours in a design that is produced by the same process with the same minimum standards, over and over. Each custom-built aircraft, on the other hand, is handcrafted with varying degrees of manufacturer (builder) skill and quality. Since they aren't built under the same watchful eye of the FAA (and an assembly-line quality-control examiner), each one is unique. This also means that each time you fly a custom-built, it's like a new test flight.

You can also join or start a flying club. Typically, a flying club is a group of people that numbers more than five and flies the same aircraft. Increasing the number of minority owners can reduce the cost per person, but it can also increase the headaches of scheduling, maintenance, insurance, and more. But there are variations in the setup of these clubs. For example, some provide equal ownership in the aircraft while others provide a small equity stake in the aircraft and offer a discounted rental rate for the aircraft. Almost all require a "buy in" or membership amount. Additionally, they usually have monthly dues to help maintain the aircraft and hourly costs to "rent" the aircraft.

But for those of us who neither want nor really need partners, but could sure use a little help in covering the costs of the aircraft, what do we do? Is it possible to share the costs with another person or persons but still own the aircraft? Sometimes, if in exchange for them paying on your aircraft they can fly the aircraft now and then. But there are a few problems associated with sharing the costs. The FAA is one. The insurance underwriters are the next. Not insurmountable, but still very important in the decision.

The FAA has guidelines that must be followed when sharing the costs or being reimbursed for the cost of the aircraft. FAR Part 91 includes a section about uses of the aircraft and charging for its use. It has always been understood and implied that this was just for fuel and oil. But often that is just not enough help to offset the ownership costs. How can a person let someone use their aircraft and only pay for fuel and oil? What about maintenance, hangar, insurance, *and* the fuel and oil costs?

What the owner might do is actually share the costs of the aircraft and charge the other pilots an amount for using the aircraft. This amount might be an hourly charge that includes the cost of fuel and oil or it might be a set amount that excludes fuel and oil.

The key here is that this might be a way to help the owner recover some of the costs of plane ownership. But you, as the owner, need to make sure that you review a copy of the agreement with the FAA FSDO in your area and your insurance underwriter prior to being paid for the use of your pride and joy. If not, you may be putting yourself in a situation of no insurance coverage because of FAR or pilot exclusions and the risk of FAA violations.

If you learn to fly in a high-wing, you'll most likely want to make a high-wing your first investment...

Personal Preferences

One of the last things to consider when buying the aircraft is your personal preference. This is where we decide what we want in an aircraft. Should the aircraft have two wings, should it be a high-wing, or should it be a low-wing aircraft? Many people have a personal opinion about each of these things. The tendency is that if you learned in a low-wing, your first aircraft should probably be a low-wing. Your comfort level is higher in an aircraft similar to the one you learned to fly in.

Another rule of thumb is that if you fly over a large amount of water, you might want a low-wing. Why? They float longer if you have to ditch in the water. If you fly over trees and mountains, a high-wing is desirable. You can see through the trees on the emergency landing. Seriously, some people like the looks of a high-wing and the visibility it offers, while others are happy with the profile of a low-wing and the visibility it offers in flight. And there are still other people who can't make up their minds and own biplanes. Two-wings are usually found in the custom-built market or as antiques. Few of these aircraft have enclosed cabins and fewer still offer the comforts of high- or low-wing cabin aircraft. But the classic design offered by biplanes is something that some people desire.

Another factor in the personal preferences (and this is not about color, avionics, and interior) is the seating arrangement. A few two-seat aircraft are designed in a tandem arrangement with one person in front of the other person. For many, tandem seating offers a "Walter Mitty fighter pilot" feel for the pilot. Some also consider it an advantageous and safer way to fly because of the visibility and "centered" feel it affords the pilot. On the negative side, a tandem-seat aircraft in which the pilot sits in the back seat puts the pilot at a disadvantage for visibility when on the ground and looking over the front of the aircraft.

...likewise, if you learn to fly in a low-wing, you'll most likely want a low-wing for your first airplane.

Chapter 2

Before You Buy

After the "inner pilot" search is completed and the decision to buy is made, it is time to select an aircraft. But first, set a few guidelines in your selection process. Remember, selection includes the buyer's personality, ownership options, etc. Now, after that in-depth soul search, it is time to select an aircraft that really meets the requirements.

As a buyer, you'll need a way to rate or categorize your selections to see if they fit your needs, skills, and budget. A basic rating system should include the cost of operation, cockpit comfort, cruise speed, useful load, and serviceability and parts availability. While you might have a few more things that you want to look for, these major items will help the average pilot make a "rational" decision—or as rational as can be. After the rational decisions are made, a personal rating system can be used to help decide which aircraft will be your personal dream plane. These ratings are a comparison of the listings used in this book.

Rational Ratings

Ratings	Low	Medium	High
Cost of Operation	★	★★★	★★★★★
Cockpit Comfort	★	★★★	★★★★★
Cruise Speed	★	★★★	★★★★★
Useful Load	★	★★★	★★★★★
Serviceability and Parts Availability	★	★★★	★★★★★

Rational Ratings

All owners are concerned about more than just the five items listed, but initially these are the most important. Yes, a buyer should be concerned with items like takeoff distances, empty weight, or even wingspan, but that will fall into the personal preferences addressed later. Each of those items (plus many others) are important for owners and should probably be considered in some fashion. But in the initial overall purchase they are small concerns. The five areas listed above, however, are initial selection criteria. If the aircraft doesn't meet those areas, the owner will definitely be unhappy. If it can't go into a couple of small private strips because of its landing and takeoff performance, it will be an inconvenience; but the aircraft will still be valuable a major percentage of the ownership time.

I should also clarify that even though the aircraft designs are based on the standard FAA pilot size, I don't think that is reality. I base my ideal characteristics on what I see in the everyday pilot. That means adults are about 190 pounds in weight; they are taking children, young adults, and friends along; and they are carrying a few items as baggage. And I don't think we skimp on baggage: I consider 25 pounds per person an average number. Sure, you can fly with less and you might be under the weight of 190, but I want an *average* profile.

Cost of Operation

Cost of operation is probably the first thing to consider. The goal of owning an aircraft is to be able to fly it. If the owner can afford to put fuel in the tanks, but can't pay the maintenance bills, then the aircraft is probably not the right one for him or her. Don't worry. This doesn't mean that you can't own what you want, but it does mean you have to decide if what you want is really the right aircraft for you! Maybe the ego side of your personality, and not the practical side, is driving the purchase. There is nothing wrong with a little ego, just as long as you can pay the bills. As we discussed earlier, the way to keep ownership costs down is to fly the aircraft.

To begin, the cost of ownership should include the direct operating cost, which includes such items as fuel and oil, and any routine maintenance required by the aircraft and its components. Indirect operating costs like engine, propeller, avionics, and airframe reserves should also be added to the direct operating costs. Additionally, the aircraft's operational costs should include the cost of purchasing the aircraft, hangar or tie-down, and insurance. Whether the aircraft was paid for with cash or a loan, there is an investment value to the money used in the purchase. It might not be critical to you, but it should be figured into the cost.

To calculate the ownership costs it's best to use a chart of some sort. Putting pencil to paper and having the numbers in black and white helps make the costs real. Many buyers try to convince themselves of the fact that all they have to do is cut down on the extra candy bar or maybe have one less dinner out to afford the aircraft. And quite a few owners calculate the cost of ownership based solely on the amount of fuel the aircraft uses. All the other expenses are left to the surprise factor. *Surprise! Your annual is due!* Cost is a part of ownership that cannot be eliminated. Owners have to live with the fact that they will be paying for the privilege of owning . . . for as long as they own the aircraft.

The cost ranking is based on five basic areas. Each aircraft is given a rating based on its fuel burn, age, construction materials, estimated average annual inspection cost, and whether it is a tri-gear aircraft.

For two-seat, fixed-gear aircraft, credit is given for having a fuel burn of less than 8 gallons an hour. Four-seat standard aircraft are given credit for burning less than 10 gallons per hour, and for four-seat and six-seat high-performance aircraft the fuel burn cutoff is 12 gallons an hour. All the aircraft are given credit if a large percentage of the models available on the used market are less than 25 years old. Old age increases maintenance costs and the overall expense of ownership. The material used in the manufacture is also considered as a way to cut costs. While tube and fabric can be easier and cheaper to repair than metal, in some cases they usually increase the insurance and require a hangar for protection. Composite is the same. Not to say that all-metal airplanes are always a better purchase, but the associated costs that go with them (hangar, ease of maintenance, etc.) are.

With two-and four-seat standard aircraft, the size of the engine and estimated annual inspection costs are based on having less than a 180-horsepower engine and a fixed-pitch propeller. The four- and six-place high-performance aircraft annual inspection costs are based on having less than a 250-horsepower engine and a constant-speed propeller.

The last variable is whether the aircraft is a tri-gear design. This might not be critical to the buyer, but the cost of insurance can increase if it is a tailwheel aircraft. Insurance underwriters usually charge a little more for tailwheel aircraft and require more training or a higher minimum number of pilot hours. Additionally, the crosswind component and the comfort of the pilot when flying a tailwheel aircraft often affect the number of flying hours the owner puts onto the aircraft. All of which increases the ownership costs.

Cockpit Comfort

Cockpit comfort should also be a factor for everyone to consider. We all think we can get something that's not quite perfect and live with it. But most often, and usually within the first few hours of ownership, we discover the disappointment and the remorse of a bad choice. But by then, it's too late!

The cockpit of an aircraft doesn't have to be loaded with extras. Leather or vinyl isn't the problem here. The covers and the colors can always be changed, but what can't be changed is the legroom, the access to the controls, or the way the pilot fits behind the yoke.

Some aircraft provide extra legroom or headroom for tall pilots, while a few offer cabin widths as a selling point. To make a good decision, the pilot has to be able to see over the panel, reach the pedals, close the doors, and be comfortable. If the cockpit doesn't offer enough room for the pilot or passenger, the flights will be short or non-existent. A great example is the Cessna 150. While the 150 is a very economical aircraft to own, it doesn't offer a tremendous amount of cabin room. The seats are limited in their adjustments fore and aft. If the pilot is over about 5-foot-10, long-distance flights are uncomfortable. That doesn't mean that the 150 is a bad choice for a tall person. Quite contrary, the 150 is one of the better all-around aircraft. *But*, it is not the aircraft for everyone.

The ranking for comfort is a subjective issue. I look at actual cockpit sizes and consider the shoulder room, headroom, and legroom as the most important factors. I also include the baggage area. The aircraft won't usually need a huge baggage area because of weight; but because most items pilots carry are bulky (duffle bags with clothes, coats, etc.).

Cruise Speed

Another important factor is the cruise speed of the aircraft. The one thing that owners always want to do is travel as fast as possible. Going from Point A to Point B is the lifelong goal of many pilots. In reality, most pilots fly within a 100-mile radius of their home airport more than 75 percent of the time. In a short trip like that, the time difference for the trip is not that noticeable and there are always trade-offs. Speed costs money, whether in the form of aircraft purchase price or fuel burn. Or, again, it might be in maintenance and insurance costs. The higher the cruise speed, the higher the cost. That's why cruise speed comparison becomes a factor in the ownership of an aircraft. Sometimes it is better to own a slower aircraft than the fire-breathing rocket that's dangerous to own and expensive to feed.

It is important to calculate the actual cost of operating each aircraft over an average flight the buyer might take. By comparing the cost of, say, a Cessna 150 and a Cessna 182, the buyer can get a good feel for the difference in per-mile cost. For example, the Cessna 150 flies at 100 miles per hour and burns 6 gallons per hour. The Cessna 182 flies at 150 miles per hour and burns 14 gallons per hour. The cost per mile for the 150 is 12 cents a mile. The basic calculations are as follows: The Cessna 150 burns 6 gallons per hour; multiply that by a $2 per gallon fuel cost. We already stated that in one hour it would travel 100 miles. If you divide the fuel cost by the miles, you get 12 cents a mile. It's the same process for the Cessna 182. The fuel burn times the cost would be $28 an hour and the Cessna 182 could go 150 miles in an hour. Divide the miles into the fuel burn and you get 18.6 cents per mile. None of this includes any set-aside for overhauls, maintenance, insurance, etc. Each aircraft would have to have those figures added in to get an actual number. But as a rough rule of thumb, this is an adequate calculation.

Although cruise speed costs money, we all want to fly as fast as possible. For that reason the ranking is based on the average book cruise speed. The faster the cruise, the higher ranking the aircraft receives. Although you have to remember that to achieve the higher cruise speed probably requires a bigger engine. For example, the American Champion Decathlon is a very fast aircraft. But it uses a 180-horsepower engine and constant-speed propeller (and also tandem seating, symmetrical airfoil, and a tailwheel configuration) to generate the higher numbers. Because of these other factors, it is not the highest-rated aircraft, even though it is the fastest two-seat!

Useful Load

If the plan is to travel cross-country or just go for the $100 hamburger, pilots hate to fly alone. And even if they do travel alone there are always a limited number of things that need to travel with them. These might include a tent, sleeping bags, or survival equipment. And whatever it is, it eats away at the useful load of an aircraft. Not only do we have to concern ourselves with the amount of fuel, but we also need to figure out who will fly with us the most, how much they weigh, and what they like to travel with. If you have two children and two standard poodles, the average four-place aircraft won't be big enough. The "useful load" is also one of the few factors that controls how far the aircraft can fly. If the aircraft doesn't have enough useful load, you might not be able to carry enough fuel, baggage, people, etc. . . . Something will suffer.

In some cases it is better to buy a lower-horsepower, four-place aircraft (a two-plus-two) that allows two larger people, and their baggage, to go on the same trip. An example might be a Cherokee 140. The original Cherokee 140s were two-seat trainers with baggage space behind the seats. The jump seats had a snap-in arrangement. They didn't provide much comfort, or room for that matter, for adults. But the 150-horsepower engine is a better performer than the Cessna 150 and the operating cost is not that much different.

I mentioned before that experience has shown that the average person is probably heavier and carries more stuff than the FAA certifications require. So in figuring the useful load, the ranking uses weights higher (190 pounds) than those devised by the FAA. Fuel is also removed from the useful load. While a factory can claim a tremendous useful load, the aircraft might have huge fuel tanks that take up most of the load. An example is an aircraft like the American Champion Citabria. This aircraft is very economical to operate and very practical in most cases, but the useful load is really low after removing the weight of the full fuel tanks. The aircraft holds 40 gallons and is powered by a

Lycoming 118-horsepower engine. Other aircraft with this engine often have less than 25-gallon fuel tanks. To really consider the aircraft as a practical two-seat (with baggage) requires flying on less than full fuel. While this is a great way to use the aircraft, the ranking is based on the standard full fuel quantities.

Serviceability and Parts Availability

It doesn't do any good to buy an aircraft that you can't have repaired at the local airport, unless you are willing to do the parts search and maintenance yourself. A good example is the Beechcraft Bonanza from the 1940s. The first model year, 1947, can be purchased at a reasonably low price (as retractable high-performance aircraft go), and the fuel burn is quite low for the cruise speeds it can attain. But the problems are parts and maintenance. While it can be worked on by most mechanics, the aircraft is difficult to find parts for. You can't afford to pay the mechanic enough to research and locate the parts at the time of the annual.

All these run-of-the-mill aircraft have lots of salvage and after-market parts available. And some of them are still in production. They might not seem "special" or "rare" except for the fact that they can be repaired!

While many people do not agree, all-metal aircraft are more popular than fabric. For this reason, the "availability of parts and serviceability" ranking gives credit for an all-metal airframe. Almost any mechanic anywhere can service a conventional all-metal aircraft. Credit is also given for aircraft that have high production numbers. The more that were built, the more spare parts that are available on the after-market and in the salvage yards.

If the aircraft model was still in production at the time of this writing (Piper Archer, Cessna 172, etc.), chances are that the factory will be able to supply parts quicker and at a lower cost than if the mechanic has to custom make them. And the fact that an aircraft is made by a factory as an FAA-certified aircraft increases its serviceability. Many mechanics are reluctant to work on custom-built aircraft. Of course, if you build the aircraft you can do the repairs. But, that's not going to be the situation when you buy a completed custom-built aircraft.

Personal Rating System

Your personal rating system should cover all the things that you want. This is also the area where you look at the actual condition, hours, use, and other factors in the decision-making process.

Personal Rating System

When purchasing an aircraft, a buyer needs to develop a personal rating system to determine the things that are important to him or her. There are a few additional personal things that most buyers will take into account like number of wings, location of wings, type of landing gear, construction materials, and cockpit layout.

Ratings	Low	Medium	High
1. Condition	★	★★★	★★★★★
2. Hours	★	★★★	★★★★★
3. Interior	★	★★★	★★★★★
4. Exterior	★	★★★	★★★★★
5. Avionics	★	★★★	★★★★★
6. Past activity or use	★	★★★	★★★★★
7. Personal needs	★	★★★	★★★★★

While condition *is* a factor, the paint and interior can be replaced. A lot depends on the buyer's ability and desire to take on a project. Many modifications, including paint and upholstery, may require an FAA mechanic's sign-off in the logbook. If that is the case, and you do not have the money or the connections to get the repairs or refurbishment done in accordance with the FAA rules, you should shop for an aircraft that doesn't need that kind of work.

While the finish is secondary, it might indicate the type of care the aircraft has received through the years. But more important is the condition of the engine and mechanical components. One factor that can affect those is the number of hours on the aircraft.

Total airframe time is typically not a problem for most aircraft. There are a few aircraft with important airworthiness directives (ADs), or service bulletins based on airframe hours, and there are a few aircraft targeted for airframe overhauls at a certain hour-life. Generally there are few, if any, limits in total hours.

In fact, the risky purchase is the old aircraft that has spent very few hours in the air. A 20-year-old aircraft that has 1,000 hours total time has more potential for dried-out gaskets and seals or corrosion on the airframe and engine parts than a 5,000-hour aircraft.

One reason I don't mind high time is that this means the aircraft was flown regularly, which usually indicates that the maintenance has been kept up. (Not always, but usually.) Past experience shows that an aircraft that doesn't fly much is prone to problems.

Dried-up gaskets, gauges, and hoses, or anything that deteriorates because of inactivity can, and usually does, go bad. After you start using the aircraft on a regular basis, you will start to replace things. Low time is like the good news and the bad news. The good news is the low total time! The bad news is the low total time! I know, many an owner will tell you how great it is to own a new or low-time aircraft. And they are probably right: it is really great to own a low-time aircraft. But we're talking cost here. If you want a good, ready-to-fly, reasonably priced aircraft, look for the higher-time airplane.

The interior and exterior of any aircraft can be modified, changed, or left as is. Again, it has to do with the amount of time and money the buyer has available to put into the aircraft. A new owner does have to be careful that he or she doesn't put too much into an aircraft. Adding new paint and interior along with an engine and all the newest avionics could push the value way past reasonable.

Avionics can cost as much as the complete aircraft. Most pilots want everything that is imaginable in the panel of their dream aircraft. But sometimes it's not possible or even rational. If you are a Visual Flight Rules (VFR) pilot with no plans of an advanced rating, buy an aircraft that has good VFR equipment installed. That usually means a communications radio, a transponder, and some form of navigation. An owner can fly from one end of the United States to the other with nothing more than a hand-held hiking Global Positioning System (GPS). The introduction of all the newest and most elaborate multi-function pieces of equipment may be on everyone's wish list, but they are not needed. Most pilots will never use all the functions these new items can do. Why waste the money on that when you can put the money into a lower-time engine?

Looking at the past activity or use of the aircraft can be important for some people; an aircraft that has been well maintained and has complete or reasonably complete logbooks should be what all buyers are looking for. But missing logbooks, a trainer history, or even a previous life as a freight hauler shouldn't detour the buyer, especially if the aircraft can meet the needs and pass the inspections and scrutiny of the buyer and mechanic.

Alternative Rating Worksheet

This evaluation form can be used to help narrow your final selection by comparing two or more aircraft on the basis of your qualifications and how you intend to use your aircraft. For the first three considerations, use the following point system: 5 points for 75–100%, 3 points for 50–75%, and 1 point for 0–50%. For the others use 5 points for "very practical," 3 points for "fairly practical," and 1 point for "not practical."

1. Percentage of past experience devoted to flying this type of aircraft: ____
2. Percentage of time you will use the aircraft for the purpose for which it was built (aerobatics, cross-country travel, local travel): ____
3. Percentage of time you intend to fully utilize passenger capacity: ____
4. How practical is it for the airport where it will be kept (runway surface, hangar, elevation)? ____
5. How practical is its annual operational cost in light of your ability or willingness to pay? ____
6. How practical is it from the standpoint of your personal preferences? ____

TOTAL ____

Don't stretch the truth in any of these areas. If it's too hard to fly or too expensive, YOU WON'T FLY IT VERY MUCH!

Chapter 3

What to Ask

When you are ready to start shopping for an airplane, you need to establish a list of questions that you can ask the seller. This list should cover not only the aircraft's specifications, but also information about who owned the aircraft, what it was used for, and where it spent most of its life. (You should also spend some time learning the lingo. The aviation industry uses a lot of abbreviations in advertisements. This chapter includes a list of the most popular.) By asking these questions a few times, you'll be able to sort through the ads and eliminate the aircraft that don't meet your expectations. These first questions will be asked of each model, because the purpose is the same: to sort through the ads and find out if the background of the aircraft is something you can accept for your dream aircraft.

When shopping for an aircraft, it's important for the physical structure to be in good shape. While many of us would turn down an airplane with paint and surface problems, it might actually be a good deal. Underneath all the bare spots and primer, there may be a solid airframe and a good first aircraft.

It's best to start with a few basic ownership questions. It's amazing how many aircraft are sold by people who aren't the owners. For this reason, it's important to find out things, like where the aircraft has been based for the last few years, when the last annual was done, and who the registered owner is. I'd also ask for an FAA registration number and look it up on the Internet; there are numerous sites that provide registration searches. This is a quick and easy way to see whom the last registered owner was. Although the FAA records are usually a little slow, it will still show if the aircraft title has changed hands recently.

Aircraft Abbreviations Commonly Used in Advertisements

The following abbreviations will be used in aircraft advertisements, manuals, and pilot operating handbooks.

Aircraft History Abbreviations

0SFRM: Zero time since a factory remanufacture
0SMOH: Zero time since major engine overhaul
FWF: Firewall forward
MDH: Major damage history
NDH: No damage history
SCMOH: Since chrome cylinder major overhaul
SFRM: Since factory remanufacture
SMOH: Since major engine overhaul
SOH: Since engine overhaul (not necessarily a major)
SPOH: Since prop overhaul
STOH: Since top overhaul (pistons, cylinders, and valve train)
TBO: Time between overhaul (factory recommendations)
TT: Total time
TTA: Total time on the airframe
TTAE: Total time on the airframe and engine
TTE: Total time on the engine
TTSN: Total time since new

Performance and Specification Abbreviations

mph: Miles per hour
KTS: Knots (1 knot = 1.151 statue miles per hour, or 1.852 kilometers per hour)
SM: Statue mile = 5,280 feet
NM: Nautical mile (1 nautical mile = 1 minute of arc of a great circle of the earth, or approximately 6,080 feet)
FPM: Feet per minute (usually regarding climb)
ROC: Rate of climb
AOC: Angle of climb
GPH: Gallons per hour
Cu. In.: Cubic inches displacement of engines
Sq. Ft.: Square feet regarding wing area
HP: Horsepower of engine
PSI: Pounds per square inch (tire and strut pressure)
Oct: Octane rating of fuel
Vis: Viscosity of oil
Fixed tri-gear: Nonretractable tricycle landing gear with a nose wheel
Ret. tri-gear: Retractable tricycle landing gear with a nose wheel
Conv: Conventional landing gear with tail wheel
F/P: Fixed-pitch (nonadjustable) propeller
C/S - Constant-speed (governed speed, adjustable-pitch) propeller
Gen - Generator
Alt - Alternator
V - Volts
Amp - Amperage of the alternator (electrical system rating)
STD - Standard fuel
L/R - Long-range fuel

If the registered owner's name is different than the person selling the aircraft, you might be talking to a dealer or broker. In some cases, buying from a dealer or broker might be in your best interest, but you need to know that up front. A broker might not know the history of the aircraft as well as the owner. Even though a pre-purchase inspection should help, the owner will offer a little more insight into the aircraft's past.

Once ownership is established, ask about the aircraft's current condition and equipment. This is when you find out how many hours are on the engine and airframe and what types of avionics are installed. This is also an opportunity to ask for pictures of the aircraft. Photos of the outside, inside, and panel should help provide a better description of the aircraft. And remember: the more pictures the better! Pictures and videos can save you money in the long run. Seeing the aircraft online or in a video prevents an unnecessary trip to see an unwanted airplane.

Where to Find an Airplane

When you have your questions figured out, it's time to start shopping. But where? There are four major choices: local contacts, direct mail, airport shopping, and classified ads. Each method can give the buyer positive results. The goal is to find an aircraft that's in good condition and can be purchased for a reasonable price.

Local contacts can often uncover good-quality aircraft from local owners. The hardest part is finding that owner (the seller). This is a referral sale: the buyer needs to contact all the aviation people in their area and let them know of their desire to purchase an aircraft. In aviation, everyone wants to make a few bucks, so don't be surprised if the referral costs you a finder's fee should you buy the aircraft.

Direct mail has been used for years in the aviation industry. Typically, the person wanting an aircraft purchases an FAA registration list of the particular model they want to buy. With Internet access, buyers can actually build a list on their own. Either way, after the list of owners is created, a postcard is sent to each one asking if he or she (the owner) is interested in selling their aircraft. Sometimes this does work, but owners receive these cards so often from dealers and brokers that they often don't pay much attention to them. Something unique or eye-catching is necessary to keep the cards from being thrown away. One idea is to make the cards from brightly colored paper and hand write the address and comments on the card. Most brokers and dealer send out pre-printed cards that are easy to call "junk" mail.

Airport shopping is one of the most fun (but also the most time-consuming and expensive) methods of finding an aircraft. This involves nothing more than flying or driving around to different airports and looking for aircraft that are for sale. This is probably the best method to find and look at aircraft. Of course, it costs time and money to travel around, but what a way to shop!

The largest and most common listings of aircraft for sale are classified ads. The classified leader has always been *Trade-a-Plane*, but the business has changed. While *Trade-a-Plane* may still be a leader, the Internet has made specialized online classifieds very popular; numerous sites have come into existence that specialize just in aircraft sales.

Internet ads have made shopping easier. A prospective buyer can access a site, sort the ads by certain criteria, and even get a preview of the aircraft through online pictures. Used to be the buyer needed the seller to take pictures and send them through the mail. Now it's nothing more than attaching them to e-mails. Not only does this cut down on time, it also helps the buyer eliminate prospective aircraft because of basic items like color, avionics, and visual condition.

The downside is speed. A potential buyer sees a nice aircraft and commits to the purchase. Buyers *do* have to be prepared to buy (seems like the "good" aircraft are always gone by the time a buyer decides to look at them), but making a snap decision without spending much time in the preview process is not advisable.

How to Establish a Value for the Aircraft

Several different values can be used: there is the book value, the bank value, the insurance value, and the price you actually pay.

The aviation business has been involved in a value growth spurt since new production stopped. In 1986, the industry decided that, since there were very few new aircraft and the market was getting smaller, prices would get higher. It's basically the story of supply and demand; we should have invested in aircraft instead of mutual funds and stocks. For years I was a registered investment advisor, and I often thought of listing aircraft as an aggressive growth investment—not for widows and orphans or retirement accounts, but for very growth-oriented investments. My first Skymaster, bought in 1992 was a 1965 version that cost me $6,500. That same aircraft now has a base value of over $45,000, and an adjusted value over $65,000.

That is a tremendous amount of growth. Could you get that from any other investment and still enjoy it?

For that reason, it is important to keep up with the value of your aircraft. Bankers and insurance underwriters usually use the *Blue Book* or *Aircraft Value Reference* Price Guide (*Vref*) to establish values. Typically, they use just the base value without the "add on" for extra equipment or hours. Often they allow only about 10 percent over the value without some sort of "proof of value," or POV.

Buyers help determine the price. No matter what anyone says, if there is not a buyer, there is not a sale. I have met many owners who said their aircraft is worth some unusually high dollar amount, but for some reason they wouldn't accept any reasonable offers. These owners advertise the aircraft, say they are going to sell, but never find a buyer that will pay their unusually high price. If you were to rely on their asking price, would it really be a fair price?

Book values can be misleading too because they are based on surveys from the subscribers and the FAA records. If the amounts are reported accurately, the prices should be correct. If, however, you own a specific model of which only two sold in the last quarter and one was in excellent condition while the other was a wreck, will that establish a fair market price? I don't think so.

As a broker, dealer, and aircraft buyer I have tried my best to purchase aircraft at the best price I can. I would like to buy every one at the lowest possible price, but that is not always possible. I do try to be comfortable with the price and I try to make the seller comfortable with the price. It's not always easy and sometimes the deal cannot be consummated. More often than not, though, the seller agrees to a fair price and it becomes a "win-win" situation. If the deal is good for both buyer and seller, the price stays reasonable, people stay in aviation, and the aircraft continues to fly!

So, how do we price an aircraft? We always get a base value. It can be from a used aircraft price book or a guide that prices the basic aircraft. Usually there are additions and subtractions for hours, condition, equipment, and other factors. This is referred to as the "book value," a good number to use for the insurance and financing companies but bad to use for your purchase price. In fact, these numbers are sometimes higher than the actual selling price. While there are always aircraft that sell at book value, there are many more that sell "below book." Most sellers start pricing and advertising at book value or above. Not surprisingly, many never get an offer.

Sample Page from *Vref*

CESSNA 152

PRICE INCLUDES: Sgl Cessna 300 navcom, 1200 SMOH, 7 P&I

Add-Ons (Ded)	$Retail	W.S.
ENG RATE	5.00	3.50
2nd navcom	1,000	700
KR86 ADF	1,200	840
Like New paint	4,000	2,800
Like New int	3,000	2,100

Performance Specs	
Config	Sgl, pst, fxd gr
Mx sts	2
Mx T.O. wt	1670 lbs
Cruise	107 knots
Range	545 nm
T.O. run	725 ft
Lndng roll	475 ft
Wing span	32 ft
Length	24 ft lin
Height	8ft 6in

Mod/Conv	Retail	W.S.

Engine

Lyc 110hp TBO 2400

O-235-L2C

Factory Reman $17,750

Average Overhaul $10,500

Market Data & Recent ADs

The good low time airplanes will bring more, but there are many below these numbers. Activity edged up from 130 airplanes 145. 4.630 are listed on the Registry. 6,628 were built. ADs = 96-09-10 oil pumps; 96-12-23

Activity: 145

Demand Rating BB

Yr	Model	Serial No	$Retail	$Trnd	$Range+/-	Whlsl	AFTT	$/Hr
78	152	79406-282031	**25,500**	↑0.5K	4,718	20.9K	7,000	.07
78	A152	A0735-080	**28,500**	↑0.5K	5,273	23.3K	7,000	.08
A=Aerobat								
79	152	82032-3591	**25,750**	↑0.5K	4,635	21.1K	6,650	0.7
79	A152	A0809-0878	**28,750**	↑0.5K	5,175	23.5K	6,650	0.8
80	152	83592-4541	**26,500**	↑0.5K	4,638	21.7K	6300	0.8
80	A152	A0879-0943	**29,500**	↑0.5K	5,163	24.1K	6,300	0.9
81	152	84542-85161	**26,750**	↑0.5K	4,414	21.9K	5,950	0.8
81	A152	A0944-0983	**29,750**	↑0.5K	4,909	24.3K	5,950	0.9
82	152	85162-594	**27,000**	↑0.5K	4,320	22.1K	5,600	0.9
82	A152	A0984-1014	**30,000**	↑0.5K	4,800	24.5K	5,600	1.0
83	152	85595-833	**27,750**	↑0.5K	4,301	22.7K	5,250	1.0
Eng Exchange to O-235-N2C. 180hp.								
83	A152	A1015-1025	**30,750**	↑0.5K	4.766	25.2K	5,250	1.1
84	152	85834-939	**29,000**	↑0.5K	4,350	23.7K	4,900	1.1
84	A152	A1026-1027	**32,000**	↑0.5K	4,800	26.2K	4,900	1.2
85	152	85940-86033	**32,500**	↑0.5K	4,713	26.6K	4,550	1.3
85	A152	A1028-1049	**35,500**	↑0.5K	5,148	29.3K	4,550	1.4

CESSA 152 Vref Vol 98-1 Page **50**

TURBINE

The *Aircraft Value Reference* Price Guide follows the *Blue Book* pretty closely. I like the different specifications and data the *Vref* offers, including, airframe hours, engine hours, airframe and avionics options, features, and condition. There is also a market range given for that special, once-in-a-lifetime, perfect aircraft. While these extras allow the price to be adjusted for any factors you can think of, it also makes the prices more subjective than those in other price guides.

Book values are often artificially high compared to actual market values. Certain specialty aircraft might be accurate, but in general, it seems that aircraft sell closer to their base values (plus or minus the engines hours).

Beside book values, you can use trade papers to get current advertised prices. These won't guarantee

General book-price increases on some aircraft may not be representative of the whole market, and vice versa. In one quarter of the year, the pressurized Skymaster increased in value $7,000, but only two aircraft were recorded as being sold. That means the price increases were based on only the two aircraft that were sold (which were unusually high priced Riley conversions), while over 10 pressurized Skymaster aircraft were listed for sale.

the values, but the ads will help you stay within the market range. You need to compare the prices in all the trade papers. This can take a little time and money, but is well worth it in the end. By calling and talking to sellers, a buyer can establish equipment, condition, and hours for the average aircraft of the type he or she is looking for. The buyer can then access any of the pricing guides on the Internet and compare the book values with the aircraft for sale.

How do you roughly establish what the market value of an aircraft should be? Start with book values (from sources like the Blue Book and Value Reference Guide). Light single engine aircraft airframes are worth about $3-4 an hour. The typical guidelines are to figure about 200 hours a year, since manufacture, for the airframe total time. Trainer, charter or commercial use aircraft usually have more hours per year, about 500. If the airframe hours are over the 200 hours per year for non-commercial use, you deduct the hourly dollar amount to the book value.

For example: A 10 year old aircraft should have 2000 hours on the airframe (200 hours times 10 years). If it has 2300 hours on the airframe, you would take $4 per hour times the 300 hours over the 2000 average. That value of $1,200 is subtracted from the book value. If the book value of the aircraft is $20,000, the adjusted price (based on 2300 hours) would be $18,800.

The same type of calculation is used for establishing the market value of the engine. Typically, the book value is based on engine hours at 50% of the TBO. Like the airframe, you add the hourly dollar amount for hours under the 50% mark and deduct for hours over 50%. Example: an engine with a 2,000 hour TBO would have a book value based on 1,000 hours since overhaul. If the engine is actually 1,500 hours since overhaul, and if you figure about $6 per hour for 4 cylinder engines, the book value would be reduced by $3,000 (1500–1000=500 times $6).

There is no one correct way to price an aircraft, but nobody likes to pay more than they should. How do you avoid this? With a lot of research. Don't hurry. And once you find an aircraft, compare its condition and price to as many other similar aircraft as you can. Call on lots of ads, research the Internet, and compare the market prices—then decide how much you think it is worth. And one last thing: never pay more than you *feel* is right.

Aircraft Financing

Dream planes don't come cheap. If you are the type of person who is buying an aircraft for personal use (which is probably 95 percent of buyers), the money is probably coming out of your "discretionary income" account. That's the extra stuff you have burning a hole in your pocket every month—the money we spend on the things we really don't need but want. Don't get all uptight and try to tell everyone how important an aircraft purchase is or how badly you need it! It may be *necessary*, but it's not *rational*! Buying an aircraft is a very emotional decision. Look at the Cessna ads—they're all emotion and fun instead of business and practicality. Since an aircraft is extremely difficult (if not impossible) to rationalize, you need to think of the money that you spend as fun money or maybe a stock market account. And remember most aircraft increase in value better than blue-chip stocks.

If you have to buy (and it is always a *have* to), you need to come up with the money. Either you dig into the savings accounts or you borrow money from a lending institution. (Or you've got the money stored in your mattress.) Do you need to finance? That's really a personal decision. Many good aircraft deals were missed because my funds were tied up in the wrong place (food, housing, clothing, etc.).

But borrowing money can sometimes be the right means to the end! Financing comes into play when you need to preserve your existing cash or when you need cash to begin with. It's even been said that another good reason to finance is because the average aircraft is only owned for a few years. Why tie up your own money in the equity in an aircraft that you don't plan to own for a very long time?

Where will you go for the money? After you've exhausted all your friends, relatives, and neighbors, you can go to your local bank, credit union, or savings bank and ask for an aircraft loan. In fact, most aircraft-lending experts recommend that you check there first. It may be easier to get a local loan because of the existing banking relationship the buyer has with the institution, but most local banks are not fluent in aircraft. If the loan officer doesn't bust out laughing, you might have a chance. If he or she stares glassy eyed, start looking elsewhere.

While a local bank may offer limited financing, they are more likely to finance on a personal signature note or use collateral that they are familiar with, like homes, cars, or equipment. Few small banks are comfortable lending on aircraft unless they are comfortable with you personally or have access to the rest of your assets. Some people have borrowed against the equity in their home. On one hand, this can offer some tax advantages. On the other hand, one should be careful borrowing against their residence for a frangible purchase. Betting the house on a commodity that can lose almost its complete value in the failure of one part, like the engine, is an awfully big risk.

Information Typically Requested on a Financing Application

Purpose of loan - Circle One	Aircraft Purchase	Avionics	Refurbishing	Engine Overhaul	Refiance
In what name will the aircraft be registered?				Total Sale Price	______
What will your Aircraft primarily be used for?	Commercial	Personal	Business	Trade/Down Pymt	– ______
Make	Model			**Financing Required**	______
Year	Serial #	Reg #			
Avionics	Total Frame Time	SMOH			
Auto Pilot	Annual Inspection Date			# of Months Requested	______

The ability of the local lending institution is also hampered by their lack of aircraft knowledge. When that engine overhaul comes due or that complete set of instrument flight rules (IFR) radios is desired, many local banks won't be receptive to increasing their loan amount. They really don't understand the increase in value associated with upgrades and repairs. Another negative is that the terms of the loans will probably be shorter. Not being experienced in aircraft lending, many small lenders treat them like cars and provide loans of five years or less.

So where is the next place to look for an aircraft loan? An aircraft lending specialist! This could be a loan broker, someone who has developed a relationship with numerous lending or financing organizations. This relationship allows the broker to collect all the necessary information and oftentimes do the credit checks before he or she presents a loan application to the lenders. Loan brokers make their money from points, which are percentages or fees established by the lenders. They are in the aviation business to make money, although many might see it as impossible. Don't expect them to find you a loan for free! Many loan brokers in aviation have aviation *and* banking experience (what better combination?), and oftentimes can find a place to source loans that other lenders have turned down. This is not a financing avenue to be ignored, although it is recommended that you get references.

In addition, many large national financial institutions have aviation divisions. These lenders have taken it upon themselves to offer aviation financing at affordable rates for extended terms—and the people who underwrite the loans know airplanes and aviation. These institutions also provide all the assorted support services needed for aircraft loans, such as title searches and escrow accounts.

What things should you consider when looking for a loan? First you need to decide what is of greatest importance to you. Are you looking for a longer term so that you can have lower payments? Or do you want to put less down so that you can have more money to purchase a higher-priced aircraft? Or do you want a short term and large down payment for the lowest rates possible?

After making that decision you need to think about the rates or financing charges added to the loan. The two basics types of financing are fixed-rate and variable-rate loans. Generally, fixed-rate loans have a little higher interest rate, but the rate is guaranteed to stay the same for the duration of the loan. In high inflationary times a fixed-rate loan locks in at a lower rate; no matter how the rates change with inflation, your loan payments don't change.

With a fixed-rate loan, make sure that there aren't any "balloon" payments or "call dates." The latter are dates in the future when the lender can request that the remainder of the loan be paid off completely. The former means you might make payments based on a 20-year fixed-rate loan (which are lower than on a five-year loan) but agree to make a balloon payoff at five years. Perhaps you're playing the odds that you'll win the lottery, collect a great big inheritance from the uncle you didn't know, or maybe move up the ladder at the office. Of course it could also mean that you have a certificate of deposit coming due at the same time as the balloon payment and you're planning on paying off the loan anyway.

Adjustable rate loans have interest rates that begin very competitively and are usually, in fact, lower than fixed rates. This provides the borrower an opportunity to have lower rates in the beginning of the payoff period, but with the added risk of the rates increasing with inflation. Theoretically, the rate could also decrease, but don't bet the farm on it!

If you get involved in a variable-rate or balloon loan, make sure you ask a few questions: First, ask what the rate's ceiling and floor are. Second, ask what the rate is tied to and try to avoid any rate that is determined by the market value of an aircraft. As we've already learned, those fluctuate quarterly and have never been very reliable.

It is also very important to consider all of the additional charges and fees included in a loan. When you borrow money, some companies have application fees, "points," prepayment penalties, and more. All of these add up in the total cost of the loan. You might get a lower rate but end up paying more because of the extra fees.

Rates also change because of the type and age of the aircraft. Some companies are hesitant to finance older aircraft built before, say, 1967. Others won't finance anything with fewer than two engines, while some prefer turbines only. One lender won't finance anything that the principals can't fly home if needed because it saves on repossession costs!

Rates also change because of the size of the loan. Usually, the more you borrow the cheaper it gets. Lenders have guidelines here as well. Some of the more specialized lenders lend only on amounts of $50,000 or higher. That means that buyers of small, low-priced aircraft need to go to large national companies or stay with local funding. Before you put the deposit on that used "Wingzing 2000," make sure the lender will provide the loan!

What kind of information does the lender need? Besides your next of kin and blood type they usually want a credit application, personal financial statement, proof of income, and all the aircraft information. The lender wants to find out if you are a good credit risk.

Six Basic Steps to Getting a Loan

1. Choose a financial institution that understands aircraft and aviation.
2. Select an aircraft that fits your needs and budget. Be realistic!
3. Review your credit history prior to applying for a loan. Make sure your information is current and correct.
4. Put together a complete financial package that includes a detailed loan application, an up-to-date personal financial statement, and at least two years of income verification (W2s, payroll stubs, tax returns, and business tax returns if self-employed).
5. Provide a thorough description of the aircraft, including logbook copies, airframe and engine hours, equipment lists, the results of a pre-purchase inspection, and pictures.
6. Explain how the aircraft will be used, its estimated hours of use, the location of its home base, and any other relevant details.

To do that they have to check out various areas of your personal and business lives. They look into your job or career and how long you've been at it. If you're the type that leaves a job behind like yesterday's newspaper . . . well, don't worry, they also look at other areas—things like whether you own your home and how long you've lived there. They also examine your income and cash flow and compare them to your debt. Some companies use only a debt-to-equity ratio. The maximum seems to be about 38 percent. Simply put, this means that your debt is 38 percent of your income. Others use the debt-to-equity ratio *and* a cash-flow analysis.

The borrower's past credit is also checked. Credit payments, existing accounts, and credit limits are all used in the final calculations. They also throw in a few more items, like how much money you have in the bank, what types of investments you have, and what your net worth is. This is all determined through a personal financial statement.

While the loan underwriter is collecting all this information, he or she needs to make sure that the borrower is not stretching the numbers—you know, "creative accounting." So your income is verified either through wage records or tax returns. If you're self-employed, you'll have to provide tax returns prior to final approval. The self-employed also need to show some sort of a track record in their business.

All of this seems like it could take days to complete, and in the past it did. But the research and preliminary loan approvals or declinations can now be completed in a matter of minutes. Most lenders are able to take the underwriting information over the telephone, run the credit reports, and make a preliminary decision in less than 10 minutes! And even with overnight mail and fax machines, the loan process can be completed in a matter of hours or days.

But they won't loan you the money for free! Even though lenders will pre-approve you for a certain amount of money, they still need to know the aircraft information. (Getting pre-approved is a great way to go. Let the lender tell you how much money you can borrow and then find the airplane that fits that price range.) When you're talking about aircraft, lenders get kind of picky. They like to see all the logbooks. They also like to know that its inspections are up-to-date and that it is airworthy. Finally, the lenders also want to know about the hours and equipment. Underwriters are interested in making loans on aircraft that are worth what they are lending.

Even with all this information, loan approval is still not a sure bet. As one lender stated, "The condition at the time of the loan is just a 'snapshot' of the aircraft." What he meant was that in just a day, the aircraft could go "out of annual" and become worth less than it was the previous day. All of this information needs to be taken into account to establish a value that is comfortable for the lender *and* the borrower. Typically, the *Vref* or the *Blue Book* is used as the starting point. For that reason it's important for the lender to see the actual purchase agreements. Many times, the actual sale price is lower than the "book" loan price, in which case the lender could theoretically loan 100 percent of the book price. Lenders don't like to do that. Usually they want the buyer to put a little money into the deal. That's why most loans require a 10 to 20 percent down payment.

Lenders also don't like to give loans for aircraft that will be used outside of the United States or for unique and hazardous flights. Commercial, leaseback,

AIRCRAFT PURCHASE AGREEMENT

To: Date: ____________

PLEASE ACCEPT OUR OFFER TO PURCHASE THE AIRCRAFT PRODUCTS AND/OR OTHER ITEMS SPECIFIED BELOW SUBJECT TO THE TERMS AND CONDITIONS SET FORTH IN THIS ORDER. INCLUDING THE TERMS AND CONDITION ON THE REVERSE SIDE:

YEAR	MODEL	FAA NUMBER	AIRCRAFT SERIAL NUMBERS	ENGINE SERIAL NUMBERS

SPECIFICATIONS:

TOTAL SELLING PRICE	$	
DELIVERY COST		
STATE AND LOCAL TAX		
LICENSE, TRANSFER, REGISTRATION		
TOTAL SALE	$	

CASH DEPOSIT WITH ORDER	$	
TRADE IN		

TOTAL CREDIT SALE		
CASH DUE ON DELIVERY		

CASH DUE ON DELIVERY: ____________

TRADE-IN INFORMATION

MAKE MODEL ____________

REG. NO. ____________ SER. NO. ____________

HOURS: AIRFRAME ____________ ENGINES ____________

☐ USED AIRCRAFT — Purchaser acknowledges that he has read and understands all the terms and conditions set forth on both sides hereof. Seller hereby expressly DISCLAIMS ALL WARRANTIES, whether express or implied, INCLUDING ALL IMPLIED WARRANTIES OF MERCHANTABILITY, FITNESS or otherwise in connection with this sale.

☐ NEW AIRCRAFT — PURCHASER ACKNOWLEDGES THAT HE HAS READ AND UNDERSTANDS ALL THE TERMS AND CONDITIONS SET FORTH ON BOTH SIDES HEREOF AND THE APPLICABLE NEW AIRCRAFT WARRANTY (AND ANY PASS THROUGH WARRANTIES REFERENCED THEREIN) TOGETHER WITH THEIR LIMITATIONS AND EXCLUSIONS, ALL OF WHICH ARE A PART OF THIS PURCHASE AGREEMENT JUST AS IF FULLY SET FORTH ON THE FACE PAGE HEREOF.

SELLER

Company: ____________

Address: ____________

City/State/Zip: ____________

NOT BINDING UNTIL ACCEPTED BELOW

By: ____________ Title: ____________

PURCHASER

Signed ____________

Name ____________

Address: ____________

City/State/Zip: ____________

By: ____________ Title: ____________

118-27

and rental aircraft are a little harder to finance and usually incur higher rates and shorter terms.

So We Got the Price and the Loan. What's Next?

A title search! The FAA has the habit of transferring registrations on aircraft without regard to liens or loans. Most financing companies will provide title searches. If not, the buyer can have a title search done through any number of companies that charge anything from $40 up. Without a clear title and an appropriate chain of ownership, the lender is not going to fund the transaction.

And speaking of funding, how does the seller get paid? Most lenders require the buyer to get the pre-purchase and the bill of sale before they will send the money to the seller. That makes this a Catch-22 transaction. The seller doesn't release the aircraft without the money and the lender doesn't release the money without the aircraft and bill of sale. A standoff occurs. One way around this is to view the aircraft, do the pre-buy inspection, and make the decision to accept the aircraft. At that time you contact the lender and they wire the money to the seller's bank. On receipt of the money, the seller releases the aircraft to the buyer and the deal is done. Of course, this method isn't possible on weekends or holidays.

Another option is to use an escrow account. With an escrow account, a third party holds the signed bill of sale, registration forms, and money from the lender. At the time of transaction, the papers and money are forwarded and wired to the correct parties and, *voila*, the aircraft is sold.

I'm always a proponent of obtaining professional help when buying an aircraft. And professional help usually costs a little money. But in the long run it can save you thousands. As participants in the world of aviation we all know way too much information and we try to do too much on our own, usually under the guise of saving money. If you ask most people in the world of aviation, they think "professional help" means a pre-purchase inspection. But it's much more than that. Professional help can include: an aircraft finance company from which to borrow the money, an aircraft insurance agency to provide the best quotes, a certified flight instructor qualified to give the new owner the required training, a qualified mechanic to perform the best possible pre-purchase inspection, and a title search company to make sure the paperwork is done correctly. Oftentimes, the escrow company that holds the money and papers is able to provide a title search as well.

Did We Forget Something?

Prior to leaving with the aircraft, the seller has to make sure the aircraft is insured. Two questions many people ask are, "Why should I buy insurance? Is it required?" A few states have started to require liability coverage, but most states don't require insurance. Most finance companies also require insurance coverage if you borrow their money, and recently there has been an increase in the number of airports and municipalities that request proof of insurance if you want to base your aircraft at their airport. So yes, a few owners are told that they must have insurance. But typically it's only for liability and only if they want to be based at a specific airport.

One way to think of insurance is in a negative light—as a necessary evil. Another way is to think of it in a positive light—as a savings account for if or when you have an accident or incident. Yet another approach is to be technical and think of it as risk management.

Possibly that's the best way to think of insurance: a means of managing financial risk. There are professional risk managers who can evaluate your risk exposure and make recommendations for your particular situation. What *you* need to do is learn a few basics. (But never pass up professional help from a risk manager if you can get it.) Managing risk can be summarized by four different actions: avoiding risk, reducing risk, containing risk, and transferring risk.

The first thing many people think about is avoiding risk altogether. One of my favorite lines is, "Flying is not inherently dangerous, crashing is!" So, what we do as pilots is not a high-risk venture until we crash, right? Seriously, if you are going to own an aircraft and fly, there is a risk associated with that activity. And the risk doesn't stop with the aircraft's value. I have had a number of people say they aren't concerned about the loss of the aircraft. They just avoid any high-risk flying: they don't fly at night, they don't fly in high winds, and, my favorite, they have lots of hours and they know how to handle the aircraft.

These are all great excuses until that one unexpected experience. It might be a time when the brakes fail or the landing gear pump quits or the main tire blows out. Then you find out how good a pilot you really are. Even though you, as the pilot, avoided the risk, the aircraft didn't. An airplane is a mechanical device that suffers wear and tear and the potential for failure. Because of that, it is very difficult to avoid the risk unless you don't fly at all. And, if you're like me, not flying sends you into withdrawal pains like most people wouldn't believe. I have never met anyone that has been able to turn off the flying bug cold and not miss it. Avoidance is very difficult.

While you may not be able to *avoid* the inherent risks of aviation you might be able to *reduce* the risks associated with flying. Maybe you could attend the "Wings" programs, get a few hours of dual instruction every month, attend recurrent training, or get an advanced rating. While there are any numbers of ways to reduce the risk, they don't *eliminate* the risk. And don't think that flying less is better. Aviation is one of those activities in which you actually increase your risk by participating less. Flying safety is improved by flying more. Being prepared for the unexpected takes practice. This is the perfect excuse to fly: to be a better, safer pilot and reduce your risk.

Sometimes "containing" the risk is explained as a version of "self-insurance." You know there is a risk in the activity and you are willing to take the responsibility for the accident. When it comes to replacing the aircraft, it might be easy for most people. But when it comes to liability, few can afford to have their pocketbook ransacked by a bunch of legal decisions in a courtroom.

If you can't afford the responsibility of the risk on your own, maybe you should transfer the risk to someone else. In fact, that seems like a great idea: chip in a little money each year to a company that promises (in writing) to pay for any damages that you might suffer during the year. While it seems like you are putting your money into someone else's pocket, remember that if you have an accident, they, not you, will pay for the claim. Hey, that sounds a lot like an insurance policy!

There is a lot more to the process, but the basic concept is that several aircraft owners pay their premiums to the insurance company and if one has an accident and needs someone to pay for the repairs or claims, the insurance company will. The insurance company is betting that the owners will collectively pay them more money than they will have to pay out. (This is probably one of the few times that the only

If you can't afford life's unexpected events, self-insurance isn't for you—you may want to consider buying insurance.

way you "win" is for something bad to happen!) The owners transfer the risk of accidents to the insurance company for a price!

Because the insurance company lets you transfer the risk to them for a very small amount of your money, they ask you to meet certain requirements. You can't expect the insurance company, for example, to ignore the fact that you are a single-engine pilot buying a big, twin-engine turboprop. They have a lot of money at risk if you make a mistake and they don't like to lose money. So don't expect them to let anyone fly anything without training and premiums. In fact, they also use risk-management steps when evaluating you. If your past experience on a particular aircraft is bad then the decision is made to avoid the risk by declining to quote or reduce the risk by requiring training, instrument ratings, or hours, or even by transferring the risk to another company that backs part of the policy. Everyone is using a version of the same process because we all want the same results: lower costs and lower risk.

Flying is a fun activity. It shouldn't be stressful. But fear of the unexpected is always there. And the unexpected *does* happen. So we need to be prepared. We need to do all we can as pilots to protect ourselves through training and risk management. Who would have thought that risk management was a way to make flying more enjoyable? But it can be. By transferring risk to the insurance company and reducing risk by increasing your abilities, there are fewer worries while you're in the air.

Basic Pre-Buy Tips

If you want to save money in aircraft ownership you need to make sure that the aircraft you buy is a good deal. And a good deal is more than just a good price.

Damage history shouldn't necessarily deter you from buying an airplane. While an aircraft's airworthiness should not be affected if it was correctly repaired and the proper records maintained, its market value may.

It's highly recommended that you use a certified mechanic for a pre-buy inspection.

Each new purchase needs to be in good flying condition with little or no work needed, *or* the price needs to reflect the aircraft's flaws (gig list). To find the flaws you need to look at the aircraft *before* you pay your money.

It's never a good experience to bring an aircraft home and have to fix a number of things that you could have noticed before you bought it. The added expense weighs not only on the pocketbook but on family relationships and friendships. Pre-purchase inspections, or "pre-buys," are a valuable way to curb unexpected surprises. Yes, pre-buys *do* help support your local mechanic, but far less than do aircraft that are bought without being inspected!

If your goal is to buy an aircraft to fly it, you definitely don't want it spending all its time in the shop. Nor do you want to spend all of your time trying to make the payments for the repairs. You bought it to fly, right? So start from the beginning and make sure that you get a good, thorough pre-buy inspection.

This doesn't mean you have to hire a mechanic, although I always recommend a mechanic who knows the type of aircraft or construction. It does means that you need to make an inspection with detached emotions. Pick the aircraft apart in your mind and be prepared for all the gigs you might find. If there are too many, stop! You don't have to buy the first aircraft you look at.

Where to start? What keeps the aircraft in the air? What complex component costs as much as the aircraft itself? The engine does. With a part that is so important and so expensive, it is in the buyer's best interest to start there.

Since an aircraft's engine is the most critical and valuable part of the aircraft, your pre-buy inspection should start there.

Whoever does the inspection should first inspect the engine for metal particles, compression, and airworthiness directive (AD) compliance. The AD list is the easiest but the most time-consuming. In theory, each individual component in or on the engine can have its own ADs. A list of serial numbers for all the accessories and parts is needed for the research to begin. Each part needs to have the records researched and compared to the applicable AD list and a note made for the records. If the ADs are not complied with, the aircraft is not flyable. If the ADs are not done, the price needs to reflect that.

What about ADs on non-certified or experimental aircraft? Theoretically, if the part is certified and the data plate stating that it is certified is intact, the ADs need to be completed. Of course that means if you are buying a certified aircraft, or one with certified parts, the ADs need to be done!

Engine inspections are a little easier. The first thing to check is the oil. The cost of buying an oil change and

What Should a Pre-Buy Cover?

Powerplants

Metal in the Oil. If there is metal in the oil, stop right now. This can be an expensive or cheap fix, but don't take any chances. If the oil was changed less than five hours ago there is no real way to tell if it contains metal; it needs at least 10 hours of operation to be accurate. Still, you want to cut the filter or check the screen. This will be at your expense. Oil analysis is also an excellent test, but it takes a longer time to get the results.

Cylinder Compression. Make sure the compression is at least 80 percent of the top compression (64/80). It can be lower, depending on engines, but most factories recommend the 80 percent rule as a minimum. Big cubic-inch Continentals can go as low as the 50s if there is no leakage past the valves.

Propeller Nicks and De-Lamination. The problem with propeller(s) is that you won't really know if it is out of limits unless it goes to a prop shop. Look at the condition and logbooks to see if there is any hint of damage or repairs.

Airworthiness Directives. If the aircraft is certified, all ADs and service bulletins should be complied with. If it is an experimental aircraft they might not be required, but they still shouldn't be ignored. ADs and service bulletins are there for a reason!

General Maintenance. A well-maintained aircraft should provide lower operating costs and safer flying.

Airframe

Corrosion. Check out the spars and spar caps, tail section, and low areas like the aircraft belly and the tail feathers. If it's just surface corrosion, and not too deep, it can be okay. If it is inner-granulated, it can be bad and an expensive repair. A good, knowledgeable mechanic can be a great help with this.

Wood Damage or Moisture in the Wood. This can be an expensive repair or replacement. Check the wing tips and low areas of the aircraft by squeezing the wood parts or tapping them with a small hammer or mallet. If you can, try a punch test for rot. Be careful not to destroy the part!

Fabric Condition. This needs to be inspected for cracks, sags, or odd-looking areas. If possible, the fabric needs to be punch tested.

Welds. Should be smooth, uniform, and penetrating. Bad-looking welds might indicate poor repairs or construction.

Riveting. Should look neat and even. Check for surrounding damage or pinched areas.

Fitting Construction. Should be neat and robust, not corroded.

De-Lamination of Components. Includes separating materials, showing fibers, or chips.

Bubbles or Cracks in Finish. Might indicate stress spots, poor assembly, or possible hidden damage.

Internal Lines or Color Change. In composite, metal, or wood can indicate stress lines or weak and damaged areas.

Overall Quality of Workmanship. The FAA offers the *4313 Guide to Repairs and Construction*, a manual that all aircraft owners should have in their possession. This manual describes and shows what types of materials, hardware, and workmanship are acceptable to the FAA.

filter or just the filter and a few quarts of oil is a lot better than buying an aircraft with a bad engine. What are you looking for in the oil? You're looking for metal particles that have departed any of the internal parts and are caught in the filter or screen. Many times a buyer will save thousands of dollars in the long run with a little cost in the beginning. I had a customer who wanted to buy a pressurized twin-engine aircraft located across the country from his home base. His mechanic had never worked on the same kind of aircraft and the buyer was concerned about the pre-buy. The aircraft was advertised with less than 200 hours on each engine.

I helped him find an experienced mechanic who flew to the aircraft and made the decision to check the filters first. His inspection found ferrous metal in both engines. The mechanic called the buyer, explained the situation, and recommended re-negotiating (unlikely at the price it was selling for) or discontinuing the purchase. The buyer opted for the latter. The mechanic cost the would-be buyer some expense but saved him costly engine problems in the long run. The unfortunate part of the story was the fact that if the next potential buyer didn't ask about the new filters, they probably got a clean inspection.

If the engine is due for an oil change, tell the seller that you'll pay the cost and do the oil change during the inspection. Most mechanics will agree that if the oil has less than around 10 hours on it, there probably won't be any signs of metal. If the engine has more than 50 hours since the last oil change, it's been almost too long to identify any problems. It should also raise doubts about the aircraft's maintenance program. If you have any other reservations, make sure you send the oil off for analysis.

Compression is the next thing to check. The minimum standard is to accept 80 percent of the top pressure in a differential pressure test. Most mechanics

Wrinkles, repairs, and patches usually indicate past damage. An inspection beyond the exterior by a certified mechanic may be prudent in many cases.

will test compression using 80 pounds of air pressure as the top pressure so that the lowest accepted compression can be only 64 pounds. And just because the cylinder is low doesn't mean it is bad. It might need rings, valves, or guides. A good mechanic can tell you where the leaks are by listening for an air leak. If the sound comes from the exhaust, plan on exhaust valve repair. If the aircraft has a leaking sound coming from the intake systems, the intake valves are probably bad. If the air rushes out the oil filler tube you'll need to replace the rings. And if the sound is from more than one area, expect an engine overhaul. Poor compression is really nothing more than a negotiating point in the price. But if you have poor compression *and* metal in the oil, there might be a few too many things wrong to continue the purchase.

For example, I had a buyer call me for pre-buy advice *after* he bought the aircraft. He had purchased a turbocharged twin and flown home with the seller. Not only did the aircraft use four quarts of oil in five hours, it also threw some oil on the windshield. The seller told him the rings had just been done and it would all straighten out after a few hours of flying. The buyer also stated that the boost never got above 25 inches—this aircraft should have had manifold pressure in the 35-inch range. The buyer ended up giving the aircraft back and taking a loss. When asked why he didn't have a pre-buy inspection done, he explained that the owner was a really nice mechanic who said everything was okay. This isn't to say that all sellers are trying to pull a fast one—it just indicates that a buyer should take all the steps possible to insure a good purchase.

In addition to a mechanical inspection, the pre-buy should include a title search and avionics, instrument, and flight checks. But here is the catch: *don't fly the aircraft from the left seat to perform those checks. Always let the seller make the first flights with you.* This gives you, the buyer, the opportunity to see how the owner flies the aircraft. Turn the knobs and test the radios and play with the switches. As the buyer, you're too interested in flying if you're in the left seat. All you can concentrate on is what a "great deal" the aircraft is or "how nice it will be to travel in." All the good stuff will prevent you from being rational. The right seat helps bring back a little rational thought. Additionally, if the owner won't let you fly the aircraft, don't buy it!

Any time that you buy an aircraft, your life and your bank account rely on you making a well-thought, rational decision. Using a mechanic is one way to do that. Mechanics typically do not have a vested interest in the actual aircraft. But an unbiased, experienced one can give you a pretty good estimate of your first year's maintenance costs, making the aircraft a reasonable purchase, not a dark hole in which to throw your money!

Chapter 4

Two-Seat Simple Fixed-Gear Aircraft

As discussed earlier, the best aircraft isn't always the biggest, the fastest, or even the one with the most horsepower. A case in point is the range of used two-seat, fixed-gear aircraft currently on the market; they offer a breadth of options for the prospective buyer. If you examine their specifications and ratings, you'll see that aircraft in this category can provide decent cockpit comfort, practical useful loads, reasonable cruise speeds, and relatively low operating costs—all while doing most anything the owner needs, within reason. "Within reason" are the key words. These aircraft do not have huge cockpits, wet bars, and televisions. They are small, efficient, and usually intended to be trainers—important considerations when making the decision to buy one.

Cockpit comfort varies greatly within this class. And although you might think that the decision to purchase an aircraft in this class would be determined almost entirely by the number of passengers the pilot plans to carry, that's not always the case. Because small, two-seat aircraft are usually relatively inexpensive to operate, they are tempting bargains even to those pilots who previously planned to fly with more than one passenger.

In addition to giving the pilot a "center line" view, most tandem aircraft—such as the Aeronca Champ, Aviat Husky, and American Champion Citabria—offer more leg and shoulder room than the side-by-side arrangements of other aircraft. Beware, however, that tandem seating necessitates the use of an intercom system to easily talk to your passengers. Not that an intercom system isn't useful to the side-by-side owner—it's just that it's easier to yell into the passenger's ear when you're sitting right next to him or her.

And speaking of yelling, most small, two-seat aircraft are not as quiet as their bigger cousins. A confined cockpit area and lightweight construction also mean the noise is greater. Of course, an intercom and headsets *are* a great way to counteract the noise problem whether you own a tandem or side-by-side arrangement. Not only can the pilot manage radio communications, the pilot and passenger can talk without raising their voice. It is also a safety feature, helping to prevent premature hearing loss.

But headsets *do* pose a few problems in small, side-by-side aircraft. Because space is at a premium, bumping the top or sides of the cabin isn't unusual, depending on the size of the headset and the pilot. Even colliding with the passenger is not uncommon. This is typically where a tandem seating arrangement shines—more room for each person.

Another consideration in regard to seating arrangement is that all of the tandems in this book, with the exception of the Tri-Pacer, are tailwheel aircraft. Surprisingly, tailwheel aircraft are still referred to as "conventional gear" aircraft, even though very few mainstream production aircraft are built with tailwheels. Yes, there *are* new factory and numerous custom-built tailwheel aircraft, but the production of tricycle landing gear still outnumbers the tailwheel. Plus, because wind always seems to be more of a factor in a tailwheel aircraft, the arrangement can hamper the pilot's ground handling and visibility: for a tailwheel pilot, the flight is never complete until the aircraft is tied down.

While wind is a consideration regardless of the location of your home base, those pilots who fly from high-altitude airports will find their options in this class limited. A two-seat aircraft like a Champ might be just what the pilot wants, but an airport with an elevation of 5,000 feet may very well make the 65-horsepower aircraft unusable except on the very best of days (and even then without full fuel and a passenger). And if you are thinking of cross-country travel, mountain passes will be difficult to cross with an unmodified, low-horsepower aircraft. For precisely these reasons, many of the smaller aircraft available have been upgraded with engines of higher horsepower.

But remember, power and speed cost money! Most of the aircraft listed in this section are quite economical to operate. Low-horsepower engines—with the exceptions of the Aviat Husky, American Champion Decathlon, and Vans series—burn very little fuel (relatively speaking). Upgrading to 160 to 180 horsepower might increase the speed or the climb, but the efficiency, of course, drops as the fuel burn rises. It's not unusual for a 160-horsepower engine to consume 8-10 gallons an hour.

Remember, too, what most of these aircraft were originally intended to be: easy-to-fly, economical training aircraft. From the postwar period onward, training aircraft haven't been expected to provide enough room for those long cross-countries, especially with a big load of baggage. Even though manufacturers didn't expect their trainers to be pickup trucks of the air, many pilots continue to use them precisely for that purpose. While high-horsepower examples like the Scout and Husky *are* like pack mules and allow off-road experiences better than any other aircraft in the class, useful load is, more often than not, a concern for owners of two-seaters. But if we can pack in ourselves, our toothbrushes, and a full tank of fuel, we should be happy.

The Cessna 150 is a good example of the philosophy behind two-seat trainers, and went on to become the biggest seller in aviation history. The bottom line is that any of the two-seat aircraft covered here provide a solid training vehicle and cruise speeds that still

Built from 1946 to 1949, the non-electric Aeronca Champ, with its 65-horsepower Continental engine, trained thousands of students. It is still considered a good, fun-to-fly airplane.. After 1948, the U.S. military contracted higher horsepower Champs for use as spotter planes; the engine upgrade found its way into civilian Champs through the end of production in 1951.

In an effort to make the Champ easier to fly, Aeronca added tricycle landing gear, a larger engine, and an electrical system to create the Tri-Champ. This is a 1957 example.

beat a car. Of course, the cruise speeds of the Vans series and the Decathlon are greater than those of the others, but their purchase prices are also considerably greater.

One final caveat: even if the ratings in this chapter (or anywhere in the book, for that matter) put a certain aircraft at the top of your list, it still might not be the one for you. If you can't find an acceptable example for sale, it doesn't matter how great it looks on paper. If parts or service are hard to come by, it might drop even lower down the list.

The Champ's chief competitor in the 1940s was the Piper Cub. To get a leg up on Piper, Aeronca moved the pilot to the front seat, raised the seat for even better visibility, and utilized a less-drafty, hinged door. Although Champs were non-electric, many currently on the market have aftermarket instrumentation.

A bubble windshield and lower nose also give the pilot better visibility than he or she would have in a Cub.

Aeronca Champ

The Aeronca Champ was introduced in the late 1930s as a basic trainer with a low-horsepower engine. Today, the most popular versions are the 1946 models typically using 65-horsepower Continental engines. This completely fabric-covered model rarely has an electrical system or starter. And, of course, a 1946 model is an old airplane, making a good pre-buy inspection all the more crucial.

Through the years the Champ has seen very few major improvements, other than a few horsepower increases. The most important things to look for are the addition of an electrical system and modification of the wing spars. The original Champ was built with a completely wooden wing. With more than a half-century of service to their credit, the spars are often found to have cracks and require replacement or repair.

The cost of a good Champ can be as much as a comparable all-metal aircraft that will go faster and haul more weight. But the Champ has its followers, mostly those who crave simplicity and a trip back in time.

Aeronca Champ	
Cost of Operation	**
Cockpit Comfort	****
Cruise Speed	*
Useful Load	**
Serviceability and Parts Availability	**
Engine manufacturer and horsepower	Continental 65hp
Construction	Tube and fabric
Landing gear	Tailwheel
Maximum seating	2
Gross weight	1,220 lb
Useful load	480 lb
Cruise speed	74 mph
Stall speed	33 mph
Takeoff run 50 feet	500 ft.
Standard fuel capacity	19 gal
Range	210 mi.
Fuel burn per hour	5 GPH
Last year of production	1948
Manufacturer in business?	No
Good availability?	Yes

Aeronca Chief

The Chief is the fancy version of the Champ. While both were built of wood, steel tube, and fabric, powered by the Continental 65-horsepower engine, and lacking an electrical system, the Chief featured a

Built from 1946 to 1951, the tube-and-fabric Aeronca Chief features a side-by-side seating arrangement.

The Chief also sports "modern" yokes rather than control sticks like those in Champs.

Think of American Champion's Citabria as a souped-up Champ, designed and approved for basic aerobatics—in fact, its name is "airbatic" spelled backwards. It's available with engines ranging from 100 to 160 horsepower.

Aeronca Chief	
Cost of Operation	**
Cockpit Comfort	***
Cruise Speed	*
Useful Load	**
Serviceability and Parts Availability	**
Engine manufacturer and horsepower	Continental 65hp
Construction	Tube and fabric
Landing gear	Tailwheel
Maximum seating	2
Gross weight	1,250 lb
Useful load	464 lb
Cruise speed	72 mph
Stall speed	33 mph
Takeoff run 50 feet	583 ft.
Standard fuel capacity	15 gal
Optional fuel capacity	23 gal
Range	180 mi.
Fuel burn per hour	5 GPH
Last year of production	1948
Manufacturer in business?	No
Good availability?	Yes

American Champion Citabria	
Cost of Operation	***
Cockpit Comfort	****
Cruise Speed	**
Useful Load	*
Serviceability and Parts Availability	****
Engine manufacturer and horsepower	Lycoming 118hp
Construction	Tube and fabric
Landing gear	Tailwheel
Maximum seating	2
Gross weight	1,650 lb
Useful load	530 lb
Cruise speed	94 mph
Stall speed	45 mph
Takeoff run	450 ft.
Takeoff run 50 feet	890 ft.
Landing roll	400 ft.
Standard fuel capacity	40 gal
Range	301 mi.
Fuel burn per hour	6 GPH
Last year of production	2001
Manufacturer in business?	Yes
Good availability?	Yes

The American Champion Decathlon uses 150- to 180-horsepower Lycoming engines and a semi-symmetrical airfoil on the wing to improve its aerobatic performance.

modern, side-by-side seating arrangement and the now-standard control yokes. More than 2,300 Champs and Chiefs were produced from 1946 to 1951, including a four-seat version built from 1948 to 1951.

American Champion Citabria

The Citabria and its relatives, the Scout and Decathlon, all started as advanced and improved versions of the old tandem wood-and-fabric Aeronca Champ. The Citabria was actually designed more for aerobatics. In fact, its name is a variation of the word "aerobatic" spelled backward.

Versions of the Citabria have been built from 1960 to present day. Various engines ranging from 100- to 160-horsepower are available. Don't get caught up in all the letter designations. From the 7-KCAB to the 7-GCAA and 7-GCBC, the list goes on and on. Suffice to say, each indicates a year and engine designation that takes a lot of effort to decipher. The important considerations here are the year and engine rating—the rest are just markings on the data plate.

American Champion Decathlon

Strengthened for higher G-loads and featuring a wing airfoil for better outside and inverted maneuvers, the Decathlon is the thoroughbred version of the aerobatic Citabria. While the airplane's symmetrical wing shape offers a better cruise speed and makes it more maneuverable in the aerobatic box, it also increases the stall speed slightly.

American Champion Decathlon	
Cost of Operation	*
Cockpit Comfort	****
Cruise Speed	*****
Useful Load	*
Serviceability and Parts Availability	****
Engine manufacturer and horsepower	Lycoming 180hp
Construction	Tube and fabric
Landing gear	Tailwheel
Maximum seating	2
Gross weight	1,800 lb
Useful load	485 lb
Cruise speed	150 mph
Stall speed	52 mph
Takeoff run	650 ft.
Takeoff run 50 feet	1,050 ft.
Landing roll	885 ft.
Standard fuel capacity	40 gal
Range	370 mi.
Fuel burn per hour	10 GPH
Last year of production	2001
Manufacturer in business?	Yes
Good availability?	Yes

The American Champion Scout is a bush pilot's workhorse, designed with a 180-horsepower engine, a large wing, and large flaps to enhance its off-airport capabilities.

Originally produced in 1971 with a 150-horsepower Lycoming, the Decathlon is also available as the Super Decathlon, first built in 1977 and powered by a 180-horse power aerobatic engine. This combination offers unusual speed and performance in a small but expensive package. Most Decathlons are equipped with a complete inverted fuel and oil system.

American Champion Scout	
Cost of Operation	*
Cockpit Comfort	****
Cruise Speed	*****
Useful Load	*****
Serviceability and Parts Availability	****
Engine manufacturer and horsepower	Lycoming 180hp
Construction	Tube and fabric
Landing gear	Tailwheel
Maximum seating	2
Gross weight	2,150 lb

American Champion Scout—*continued*	
Useful load	750 lb
Cruise speed	122 mph
Stall speed	46 mph
Takeoff run	490 ft.
Takeoff run 50 feet	1,025 ft.
Landing roll	420 ft.
Standard fuel capacity	35 gal
Optional fuel capacity	70 gal
Range	420 mi.
Fuel burn per hour	10 GPH
Last year of production	2001
Manufacturer in business?	Yes
Good availability?	Yes

The Aviat Husky was designed as a modern-day replacement for the Piper Super Cub. While it may look similar, the Husky offers much-desired modifications like a constant-speed propeller, a 180-horsepower engine, and flaps. The heavy-duty tailwheel landing gear makes this an off-road vehicle for the aviation world.

Bush pilots like big wheels, lots of horsepower, and practical cockpit designs. For example, many small, backcountry aircraft use a tandem seating design whenever possible. This provides a "center line" control feel for the pilot, not to mention better side visibility when landing on those off-the-beaten-path airstrips.

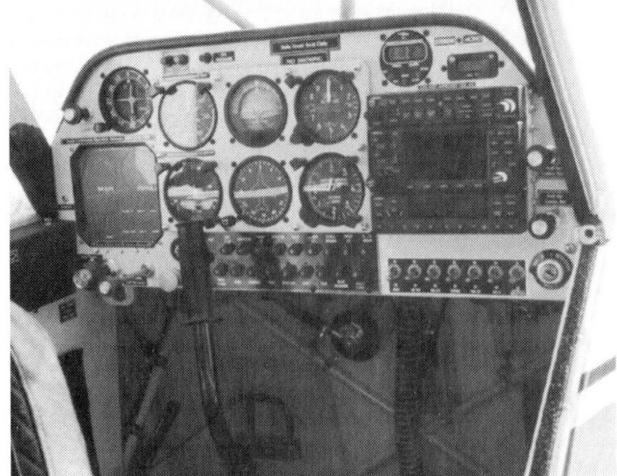

Even though the Husky's heritage is in the bush aircraft of the 1940s and 1950s, its avionics and gauges are anything but antiquated. Modern transceivers, global positioning systems, moving maps, autopilot, and multifunctional displays are regularly ordered in new Huskys and often found as upgrades on used aircraft.

Aviat Husky	
Cost of Operation	*
Cockpit Comfort	****
Cruise Speed	*****
Useful Load	****
Serviceability and Parts Availability	****
Engine manufacturer and horsepower	Lycoming 180hp
Construction	Tube and fabric
Landing gear	Tailwheel
Maximum seating	2
Gross weight	1,890 lb
Useful load	700 lb
Cruise speed	139 mph
Stall speed	45 mph
Takeoff run	200 ft.
Landing roll	350 ft.
Standard fuel capacity	52 gal
Range	686 mi.
Fuel burn per hour	10 GPH
Last year of production	2001
Manufacturer in business?	Yes
Good availability?	Yes

American Champion Scout

The Scout is the workhorse of the Champion line. With a large useful load, heavy-duty wing, and 180-horsepower engine, it is the "off-road" version of the Citabria and its lightweight variations. The Scout has been produced from 1964 to the present.

Aviat Husky

The Husky is the bush plane entry of Aviat Aircraft, best known for their Pitts Special aerobatic biplanes. The Husky basically takes everything the American Champion Scout and Piper Super Cub have to offer and tries to make them better. The "off-road" tandem-seat Husky, designed with modern avionics, a 180-horsepower engine, flaps, and short-field performance, has the ability to adapt to skis and floats, making it an all-around, backcountry, traveling machine. The Husky hit the market in 1987 and has been selling consistently ever since. Numerous used models are available. Its only real contemporary competition is the aforementioned Scout.

Beechcraft Skipper

Built and sold from 1979 through 1983, the Model 77 Skipper was Beechcraft's low-wing, two-place attempt at the trainer market. The Skipper is an economical, two-place, tricycle-gear aircraft. The easy entry afforded by its two cabin doors was somewhat of a novelty for low-wing aircraft of the period, most of which had a single door.

The Skipper also has a "T" tail that Beechcraft touted as both a performance and aesthetic improvement. There are, however, two schools of thought on the value of a raised horizontal stabilizer.

Even though the Skipper was built to the high standards of workmanship for which Beechcraft was noted, even in its day it was only an average aircraft that offered a reasonably comfortable cabin. If you find one on the used market, it might be worth looking into if you fly from a long, hard-surface runway.

Cessna 120/140

Well built and easy to fly for tailwheel aircraft, the Cessna 120 and 140 were the new trainers of the post-war 1940s. The 120 is the stripped-down version of the 140 and doesn't have any flaps or electrical system, let alone radios or much instrumentation. At the time they were introduced in 1946, their advantages were an all-metal fuselage and a fabric-covered wing since most

Beechcraft Skipper	
Cost of Operation	*****
Cockpit Comfort	**
Cruise Speed	**
Useful Load	*****
Serviceability and Parts Availability	***
Engine manufacturer and horsepower	Lycoming 115hp
Construction	Metal
Landing gear	Tri-gear
Maximum seating	2
Gross weight	1,675 lb
Useful load	572 lb
Cruise speed	97 mph
Stall speed	47 mph
Takeoff run	780 ft.
Takeoff run 50 feet	1,280 ft.
Landing roll	670 ft.
Standard fuel capacity	29 gal
Range	370 mi.
Fuel burn per hour	6 GPH
Last year of production	1981
Manufacturer in business?	Yes
Good availability?	No

competitors' were all fabric. The 120 ceased production after 1948, and the 1949 and 1950 production years were limited to the 140A, an improved version that sported an all-metal wing and single wing struts.

Things to look for in a used 120 or 140 are an electrical system (most have had one added), extended landing gear for improved ground handling, and an engine upgrade, the most popular of which is the higher horsepower Continental O-200. In addition, watch for upgrades to Cessna 150 seats and mufflers. While not necessities, they offer a little better comfort and performance. Even as stock aircraft, the Cessna 120 or 140 can be quite a value for the money—and quite a few are still on the market: after all, more than 7,000 were built during their short production run.

Cessna 150

The Cessna 150 is considered the "little trainer that could." And it did! The 150 has trained more pilots than any other aircraft. Obviously, they didn't do that by being difficult to fly or to find. The Cessna 150 began life in 1959 as "everyone's aircraft." The first 150 was a very tight (read "narrow") but efficient airplane with a straight vertical tail and slope-back fuselage. Its all-metal design and Continental O-200, 100-horsepower engine provide the aviation community with a speedy—and not too uncomfortable—cruiser and trainer. In addition, the 150's systems are simple

The Skipper was Beechcraft's two-seat trainer built from 1979 through 1983 and using the Lycoming 115-horsepower engine. The skipper competed with Cessna's 152 and Piper's Tomahawk. *Photo courtesy of* Aero Trader.

The Cessna 120 was a basic version of the 140 that offered fewer options, one of which was the lack of flaps.

Two major improvements Cessna made moving forward from the 1948 140 (seen here) to the 140A introduced in 1949, were the elimination of the double wing struts in favor of a single strut, and the switch from fabric covered wings to an all-metal design. *Photo courtesy of LeRoy Cook*

The 140A built from 1949 to 1951 was Cessna's last two seat, conventional-gear airplane. It was built with a 90-horsepower engine.

The Cessna 140 has wing flaps, one differentiation from the 120.

Cessna 120s and 140s often have after market wheel extensions that move the axle forward, increasing the distance between the front wheels and the tailwheel. The longer wheelbase is intended to improve control during takeoff and landing.

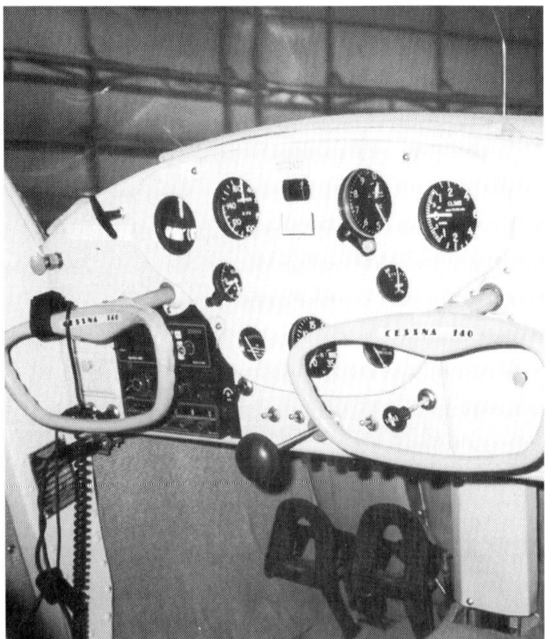

Simple, but fully equipped in its day, the 140's panel still accommodates the needs of most modern pilots.

Cessna 120/140	
Cost of Operation	**
Cockpit Comfort	**
Cruise Speed	***
Useful Load	*****
Serviceability and Parts Availability	***
Engine manufacturer and horsepower	Continental 85hp
Construction	Fabric wings; some all-metal
Landing gear	Tailwheel
Maximum seating	2
Gross weight	1,500 lb
Useful load	650 lb
Cruise speed	100 mph
Stall speed	43 mph
Takeoff run	650 ft.
Takeoff run 50 feet	1,850 ft.
Landing roll	460 ft.
Standard fuel capacity	25 gal
Range	390 mi.
Fuel burn per hour	6 GPH
Last year of production	1949
Manufacturer in business?	Yes
Good availability?	Yes

The Cessna 150 hasn't trained more pilots than any other aircraft by being difficult to fly or find.

The 150's control panel had everything the pilot needed in the late 1950s and early 1960s. *Photo courtesy of Cessna Aircraft Company*

Thinking the 150 could be used in pipeline, traffic, law enforcement, and other patrol jobs, Cessna produced a package that included larger fuel tanks and Plexiglas "observer" doors. Although this example is painted in U.S. Air Force colors, it's doubtful it actually saw any combat time.

The 152, with its 110-horsepower Lycoming engine, debuted in 1978. The airplane stepped right into the 150's shoes as one of the world's most popular trainers.

Cessna 150	
Cost of Operation	****
Cockpit Comfort	***
Cruise Speed	***
Useful Load	****
Serviceability and Parts Availability	****
Engine manufacturer and horsepower	Continental 100hp
Construction	Metal
Landing gear	Tri-gear
Maximum seating	2
Gross weight	1,500 lb
Useful load	538 lb
Cruise speed	104 mph
Stall speed	47 mph
Takeoff run	680 ft.
Takeoff run 50 feet	1,205 ft.
Landing roll	360 ft.
Standard fuel capacity	26 gal
Range	318 mi.
Fuel burn per hour	6 GPH
Last year of production	1977
Manufacturer in business?	Yes
Good availability?	Yes

and efficient. Flaps are operated by a large lever between the seats, and the landing gear are made from flat spring steel, a carryover from the 140.

But the main advantage of the Cessna 150 for pilots in the used aircraft market is in the numbers. From 1959 to 1977, the last year of production, more than 22,000 were produced. The Cessna 150 also supported a healthy after market that developed parts for repairs, replacements, and modifications. For their part, Cessna improved the 150 through the years by adding back windows in 1964, a swept tail in 1966, and extra cabin width in 1967.

The improvements continued in 1970 when Cessna offered a basic aerobatic version with caged gyros, quick-release doors, and room for parachutes. In 1971 a tubular steel gear that gave the aircraft a lower and wider stance replaced the flat-steel spring gear.

Throughout the 150's production Cessna offered options like a "kiddie's" seat mounted in the baggage area, float kits, heavy-duty nose gear, and long-range fuel capacity. Useful load, along with empty weight, also continued to increase throughout the 150's production run.

Cessna 152

The Cessna 152 was the new-and-improved version of the reliable 150. While the 150's 100-horsepower Continental has a time between overhaul (TBO) of 1,800 hours, the first 152s' 110-horsepower Lycoming engines have a TBO of 2,000 hours. Most 152s, however, have been updated with a TBO of

The 152 has enough panel space to allow pilots to update its avionics and add full instrument flight rules (IFR) instrumentation for training or functionality. The panel looks a lot like a scaled-down version of that found in its big brother, the 172.

Diamond's DA20 Katana is a two-seat trainer that utilizes modern technology; the composite aircraft offers a smooth finish, unique looks, and durability at a reasonable cost. *Photo courtesy of Norm Goyer*

Although a two-place trainer priced at six figures is understandably difficult for many to rationalize, a used DA20 can be a substantial value. *Photo courtesy of Norm Goyer*

Cessna 152	
Cost of Operation	*****
Cockpit Comfort	***
Cruise Speed	***
Useful Load	**
Serviceability and Parts Availability	****
Engine manufacturer and horsepower	Lycoming 110hp
Construction	Metal
Landing gear	Tri-gear
Maximum seating	2
Gross weight	1,670 lb
Useful load	529 lb
Cruise speed	107 mph
Stall speed	43 mph
Takeoff run	725 ft.
Takeoff run 50 feet	1,340 ft.
Landing roll	475 ft.
Standard fuel capacity	26 gal
Optional fuel capacity	39 gal
Range	315 mi.
Fuel burn per hour	6 GPH
Last year of production	1985
Manufacturer in business?	Yes
Good availability?	Yes

2,400 hours. In 1983, the 110-horsepower engine was replaced with a 108-horsepower Lycoming to accommodate the 100 low-lead aviation fuel that was available.

But talk about improvements! Not only did the book cruise speed increase from about 118 miles per hour in the Cessna 150 to approximately 123 miles per hour in the 152, so did the useful load. Of course, the cost also went up. To buy a new 152 in 1985, the last year of production, the cost was about $46,000—a lot of money for a two-place trainer at a time when the market for trainers was drying up.

Diamond Katana

Unveiled in 1995, the Katana was part of the new wave of modern trainers that featured composite construction, tilt canopies, and stick controls. Smooth, sleek, and neat looking, but priced well over $100,000, the airplane was as close to a custom-built as you could get at the time. Flight schools found the originals worked quite well, although a two-place trainer priced at six figures was, and still is, difficult for a flight school to rationalize. The replacement in 1997 of the Rotax engine with a 125-horsepower Continental IO-240 increased the aircraft's performance. As a used aircraft purchase, the Katana can offer a substantial value.

Even though the Diamond Katana is considered a small trainer or sport aircraft, its panel includes the latest avionics and can even be equipped for instrument flight.

One notable feature of Diamond aircraft is their T-tail design.

Diamond Katana	
Cost of Operation	****
Cockpit Comfort	***
Cruise Speed	****
Useful Load	*****
Serviceability and Parts Availability	****
Engine manufacturer and horsepower	Rotax 81hp
Construction	Composite
Landing gear	Tri-gear
Maximum seating	2
Gross weight	1,609 lb
Useful load	514 lb
Cruise speed	117 mph
Stall speed	37 mph
Takeoff run	1,120 ft.
Takeoff run 50 feet	1,560 ft.
Landing roll	748 ft.
Standard fuel capacity	20 gal
Range	526 mi.
Fuel burn per hour	6 GPH
Last year of production	2001
Manufacturer in business?	Yes
Good availability?	Yes

Grumman American AA1

Fun, sporty, and fast, the Yankee, as it was originally called, is a popular high-performance sports plane. It likes the runway and has an aggressive stall. In fact, it is prohibited from spins and was at one time used by National Aeronautics and Space Administration (NASA) as a test bed for spin recovery techniques. (FYI, it usually needed a parachute to recover from spins!)

The AA1 was designed by Jim Bede as the BD 1 and originally put into production by the American General Company. The production aircraft was a big step from Bede's original aerobatic, custom-built design. At the time, it was also notable for its construction, which sandwiches a honeycomb material between aluminum skins. The skins are bonded, leaving a smooth finish without rivets, edges, or sharp joints to disrupt airflow. This allows the aircraft to generate cruise speeds around 133 miles per hour—not bad for a 108-horsepower Lycoming engine! The AA1 models also have a hollow spar that houses fuel tanks which hold about 24 gallons.

The AA1 changed slightly during its nine-year run from 1969 to 1978. Typically, the modifications were designed to make the aircraft more user-friendly. The first model-year AA1 has a wing airfoil that is considered to provide much higher performance than that found on later model years. The cruise speed of the 1969 model is also better than that offered by later models, but the stall is also very abrupt—not

The Grumman American AA1 began life as the two-place, custom-built BD 1 designed by Jim Bede. In 1969, the airplane was certified by the FAA and manufactured by American General then Grumman until 1978. The Yankee, as it was called, is widely considered a hot, inexpensive trainer that offers a "fighter pilot" feel with its sliding canopy, high speed, and responsive controls. *Photo courtesy of Norm Goyer*

Getting into the cockpit of the AA1 (or the AA5, for that matter) requires sliding the canopy back, stepping on the seat, and sliding behind the controls. This cockpit is in a 1971 model.

Grumman AA1	
Cost of Operation	****
Cockpit Comfort	**
Cruise Speed	***
Useful Load	**
Serviceability and Parts Availability	***
Engine manufacturer and horsepower	Lycoming 108hp
Construction	Metal
Landing gear	Tri-gear
Maximum seating	2
Gross weight	1,500 lb

Grumman AA1—*continued*	
Useful load	493 lb
Cruise speed	109 mph
Stall speed	51 mph
Takeoff run	725 ft.
Takeoff run 50 feet	1,400 ft.
Landing roll	1,065 ft.
Standard fuel capacity	21 gal
Range	350 mi.
Fuel burn per hour	6 GPH
Last year of production	1978
Manufacturer in business?	Yes
Good availability?	Yes

uncontrollable, but the aircraft has been known to catch unsuspecting pilots by surprise. Later versions have a better airfoil but a slightly lower cruise speed. The AA1C, built during the last two years of production, uses a 115-horsepower Lycoming. More than 1,200 units were built in total. The only real difference between trainer versions (sometimes referred to as TR2s) and standard versions is the propeller: the standard aircraft offers a cruise propeller that reduces the climb but increases the cruise by about 2–3 miles per hour.

Various modifications are available, including increased fuel capacity, larger engine conversions, control sticks, and even a tailwheel. All these things are

The Taylorcraft, like many single-engine airplanes of its era, is a conventional-gear, two-seater with very little in the way of electronics or instrumentation. Most Taylorcraft airplanes came from the factory with a 65-horsepower Continental and no electrical system. Several manufacturers have tried to resurrect the model over the years, with the last production ending in 1994 with the F22C. Currently, the type certificate is owned by Airborne Marketing, Inc.

intended to make the small, bubble-canopy, castering nose wheel aircraft even more fun to fly. If you like sports cars, this could be the one for you.

Taylorcraft

C. G. Taylor is best known for designing the Piper Cub, and after that successful design he went on and developed a line of two and four seat aircraft called the Taylorcraft. The most popular were the 2 seat models, designed with a welded steel tube fuselage and wooden wings covered with fabrics. The majority of the Taylorcraft aircraft were built from 1939 until 1958. After World War II the aircraft was designated the model 19 Sportsman. The aircraft was put back into production in 1974 and built intermittently until

Piper took the Tri-Pacer design and made it into a entry-level, two-place, tricycle gear trainer. As designated by its model number (PA22-108), the Colt uses a 108-horsepower Lycoming engine. *Photo courtesy of LeRoy Cook*

Piper Colt	
Cost of Operation	***
Cockpit Comfort	***
Cruise Speed	**
Useful Load	*****
Serviceability and Parts Availability	**
Engine manufacturer and horsepower	Lycoming 108hp
Construction	Tube and fabric
Landing gear	Tri-gear
Maximum seating	2
Gross weight	1,650 lb
Useful load	710 lb
Cruise speed	94 mph
Stall speed	47 mph
Takeoff run	950 ft.
Takeoff run 50 feet	1,500 ft.
Landing roll	500 ft.
Standard fuel capacity	36 gal
Range	415 mi.
Fuel burn per hour	6 GPH
Last year of production	1963
Manufacturer in business?	Yes
Good availability?	No

With its large wing, small engine, and big tires, the Piper J3 Cub was the leading trainer of the World War II era. The large wing offers slow speeds and a light wing loading, while the design lends itself to flying from small fields and chasing the early morning sun. More adventurous pilots shortened the wing and used a larger engine to increase cruise and Maneuverability. This example is a 1946 model.

With its tailwheel configuration and the pilot soloing from the back, the worst thing about the Cub is seeing over the nose. Owners need to taxi slowly and practice their "S" turns to help avoid obstacles.

One characteristic of the J3 Cub is its narrow cowling, necessitating the protrusion of the cylinder heads.

The cockpit of the J3 Cub is the definition of simplicity—the essence of stick-and-rudder flying is from the backseat of a Cub.

In 1951, the Piper PA 18 Super Cub replaced the simple and fun J3. The Super Cub offers increased horsepower (95 to 150) and better performance. The Super Cub also handles the addition of floats—in fact, it is widely considered the original bushplane. These modifications, however, come at a cost: weight and purchase price.

Piper J3 Cub	
Cost of Operation	**
Cockpit Comfort	***
Cruise Speed	*
Useful Load	*****
Serviceability and Parts Availability	*
Engine manufacturer and horsepower	Continental 65hp
Construction	Tube and fabric
Landing gear	Tailwheel
Maximum seating	2
Gross weight	1,220 lb

Piper J3 Cub—*continued*	
Useful load	540 lb
Cruise speed	75 mph
Stall speed	33 mph
Takeoff run	370 ft.
Takeoff run 50 Feet	730 ft.
Landing roll	290 ft.
Standard fuel capacity	9 gal
Range	168 mi.
Fuel burn per hour	5 gph
Last year of production	1947
Manufacturer in business?	Yes
Good availability?	Yes

1994. The later model aircraft were called the F19, F21 and F22s and utilized engines that ranged from 100 horsepower to 180 horsepower. The most popular Taylorcraft on the used market are the models built in the 1940s.

Piper Colt

In 1960, Piper attempted to convert their reliable Tri-Pacer into an affordable entry-level aircraft. They installed a 108-horsepower Lycoming engine, listed the aircraft as a two-seater, and called it the Colt. It lasted a short three years. Corrosion in the tubing and wing struts, as well as aging of the fabric, are the Colt's biggest problems.

The Piper Tomahawk was specifically designed as a trainer to compete with Cessna's 152. It offers tricycle gear, a low-wing, and great visibility. The Tomahawk replaced Piper's previous trainer, the Cherokee, which evolved for other applications. *Photo courtesy of* Aero Trader

A distinguishing feature of the Tomahawk is its T-tail design. The T tail is less responsive at lower speeds due to its location outside of the prop blast.

Neither Colt nor Tri-Pacer resale prices have ever been strong. Still, many consider them a great buy. The key, of course, is finding a well-maintained aircraft that doesn't need to be re-covered.

Piper J3 Cub

While the Cessna 150 has generally been regarded as the world's leading trainer since the 1960s, prior to that the honor went to the Piper Cub. Constructed of wood, metal tubing, and fabric, the little Cub first hit the skies in 1939. Known as a simple and easy-to-fly two-seat aircraft, the tailwheel Cub's disadvantage is that the pilot flies from the rear seat. Nevertheless, the Cub offers a fun, albeit slow (cruising at about 75 miles per hour), ride. Figures show that 20,308 65-horsepower J3 Cubs were built through 1947, and that 4,500 are still on the FAA registry.

continued on page 72

Piper Tomahawk	
Cost of Operation	*****
Cockpit Comfort	**
Cruise Speed	***
Useful Load	**
Serviceability and Parts Availability	***
Engine manufacturer and horsepower	Lycoming 112hp
Construction	Metal
Landing gear	Tri-gear
Maximum seating	2
Gross weight	1,670 lb
Useful load	542 lb
Cruise speed	108 mph
Stall speed	49 mph
Takeoff run	820 ft.
Takeoff run 50 feet	1,460 ft.
Landing roll	707 ft.
Standard fuel capacity	30 gal
Range	384 mi.
Fuel burn per hour	6 GPH
Last year of production	1982
Manufacturer in business?	Yes
Good availability?	No

The popularity of the kit-built Vans RV 4 is largely responsible for the success of the RV 6 and RV 8 that followed. The all-metal, two-seat airplane is capable of cross-country travel and aerobatics.

The RV 4's cockpit layout features built-in rollover protection and allows the pilot to solo from the front seat.

Vans RV 4	
Cost of Operation	****
Cockpit Comfort	***
Cruise Speed	*****
Useful Load	*****
Serviceability and Parts Availability	***
Engine manufacturer and horsepower	Lycoming 160hp
Construction	Metal
Landing gear	Tailwheel
Maximum seating	2
Gross weight	1,500 lb
Useful load	596 lb
Cruise speed	193 mph
Stall speed	48 mph
Takeoff run	450 ft.
Landing roll	425 ft.
Standard fuel capacity	32 gal
Range	565 mi.
Fuel burn per hour	8 GPH
Last year of production	2000
Manufacturer in business?	Yes
Good availability?	Yes

The RV 6 provides side-by-side seating and is available in both a tailwheel version and as the RV 6A with tricycle gear. Both aircraft are designed to fly with 150- to 200-horsepower engines and can generate cruise speeds in excess of 170 miles per hour.

The RV 6 is also available in a tricycle-gear version known as the RV 6A.

The RV 6 panel provides a lot of space for avionics and a full complement of instruments for IFR use.

Vans RV 6	
Cost of Operation	****
Cockpit Comfort	***
Cruise Speed	*****
Useful Load	*****
Serviceability and Parts Availability	****
Engine manufacturer and horsepower	Lycoming 160hp
Construction	Metal
Landing gear	Tailwheel
Maximum seating	2

Vans RV 6—*continued*	
Gross weight	1,600 lb
Useful load	635 lb
Cruise speed	191 mph
Stall speed	49 mph
Takeoff run	525 ft.
Landing roll	500 ft.
Standard fuel capacity	38 gal
Range	674 mi.
Fuel burn per hour	8 GPH
Last year of production	2001
Manufacturer in business?	Yes
Good availability?	Yes

Vans RV 6A	
Cost of Operation	*****
Cockpit Comfort	***
Cruise Speed	*****
Useful Load	*****
Serviceability and Parts Availability	****
Engine manufacturer and horsepower	Lycoming 160hp
Construction	Metal
Landing gear	Tri-gear
Maximum seating	2

Vans RV 6A—*continued*	
Gross weight	1,650 lb
Useful load	665 lb
Cruise speed	189 mph
Stall speed	49 mph
Takeoff run	524 ft.
Landing roll	500 ft.
Standard fuel capacity	38 gal
Range	660 mi.
Fuel burn per hour	8 GPH
Last year of production	2001
Manufacturer in business?	Yes
Good availability?	Yes

Two of the most recent models from Vans are the RV 8 and RV 8A; the RV 8 uses conventional tailwheel landing gear while the RV 8A features tricycle gear. The RV 8 models offer more cabin space and useful load than their predecessors while maintaining the tandem seating arrangement.

As with its RV 6 brethren, the RV 8 is available in a tri-gear version known as the RV 8A. The livery on this example is evidence of Vans' role in the world's military trainer market. *Photo courtesy of William Pagan.*

Continued from page 67

Piper also offered several variations of the Cub, some modified with larger engines and electrical systems (the originals were non-electric), others with shortened wings to improve performance. The 65-horsepower J3 Cub's replacement, the PA 18 Super Cub unveiled in 1950, was built with engines rated from 95 to 150 horsepower until 1994.

The J3 Cub has been the darling of the antique airplane market for many years. Custom manufacturers have produced copycat (or copycub, as it were) versions, while ultralight manufacturers have made smaller single-seat replicas. Few, however, can generate the interest and jolt the memories of the original.

Piper Tomahawk

When it hit the market in 1978, the Piper PA-38-112 Tomahawk, with its "T" tail design, gained an unexpected reputation for shuttering or shaking during a stall. While this didn't appear to pose any safety problems, the market was slow to snap them up. Like the Beechcraft Skipper, the Tomahawk has two doors, a fairly roomy cabin, and decent performance, making it not much more than an average two-place aircraft. If you are a fan of low-wing trainers, the Tomahawk and the Skipper are nearly interchangeable. Tomahawk production grew to more than 2,500 aircraft before ceasing in 1982. Resale prices are strong, but you can usually buy a Tomahawk for less money than a Cessna 150 that's 10 years older.

Vans RV 4

One of the first designs to offer tandem seating, good cruise performance, and a tailwheel configuration, the kit-built RV 4 has won a strong following with its all-

The RV 8 panel allows more space than the RV 4 but less than the RV 6 due to the tandem seating arrangement and resulting fuselage width.

The RV 8's enlarged fuselage accommodates a forward baggage compartment.

Vans RV 8	
Cost of Operation	**
Cockpit Comfort	****
Cruise Speed	*****
Useful Load	*****
Serviceability and Parts Availability	****
Engine manufacturer and horsepower	Lycoming 180hp
Construction	Metal
Landing gear	Tailwheel
Maximum seating	2
Gross weight	1,800 lb
Useful load	710 lb
Cruise speed	204 mph
Stall speed	51 mph
Takeoff run	575 ft.
Landing roll	500 ft.
Standard fuel capacity	42 gal
Range	696 mi.
Fuel burn per hour	10 GPH
Last year of production	2001
Manufacturer in business?	Yes
Good availability?	Yes

Vans RV 8A	
Cost of Operation	***
Cockpit Comfort	****
Cruise Speed	*****
Useful Load	*****
Serviceability and Parts Availability	****
Engine manufacturer and horsepower	Lycoming 180hp
Construction	Metal
Landing gear	Tri-gear
Maximum seating	2
Gross weight	1,800 lb
Useful load	680 lb
Cruise speed	202 mph
Stall speed	51 mph
Takeoff run	575 ft.
Landing roll	550 ft.
Standard fuel capacity	42 gal
Range	687 mi.
Fuel burn per hour	10 GPH
Last year of production	2001
Manufacturer in business?	Yes
Good availability?	Yes

around performance. The pilot sits in the front seat, offering excellent visibility. Also, production numbers put a large number on the used market. As with any used aircraft, the best way to make sure an RV 4 is well built is to have a professional assist you with the pre-buy inspection. Vans' aircraft are built with conventional construction techniques that allow repair and servicing to be performed by most mechanics.

Vans RV 6/6A

The RV 6 is the side-by-side variation that replaced the popular RV 4. Again, construction is straightforward and uncomplicated, making for a nicely performing aircraft. The RV 6 is also available in a tricycle-gear version designated the RV 6A. Many of the used examples available use 150- or 160-horsepower Lycoming engines. A few have been upgraded to a 180-horsepower version with a constant-speed propeller.

Prices vary tremendously on used custom-built aircraft. Most of the value is given to the cost of parts (engine, kit, avionics, etc.), with a small amount of value given to the actual labor required to build the aircraft. Still, when nicely equipped, a used RV 6A can bring better than $60,000.

Vans RV 8/8A

The Vans RV 8 is available as both a tailwheel and as a tri-gear, designated the RV 8A. Either way, you get an enlarged tandem-seat aircraft designed for engines up to 200-horsepower and cross-country cruise speeds around 200 miles per hour. In addition, the aircraft has plenty of interior room and an extra baggage area in front of the cockpit. Yes, it is a tandem reminiscent of the RV 4, but if you are looking for speed and comfort, the RV 8 will have it. Finding one will probably take a little longer than normal—most people who build them don't want to give them up.

Chapter 5

Four-Seat Simple Fixed-Gear Aircraft

Sometimes a two-seat aircraft just won't do. Maybe family size requires a bigger aircraft, or airport elevation just makes smaller, lower-horsepower aircraft impractical. Whatever the reason, four-seat, fixed-gear aircraft have been the mainstay of the single-engine market. Most pilots can remember that very first flight after they received their private license. Whether they trained in a two-seat Piper, Cessna, or Beechcraft, that first flight was usually in a four-place aircraft: it was the next logical step after a two-seat trainer. With more room, the pilot could take a few friends or family along. Bigger was better and bigger offered more opportunities. The problem was, bigger also cost more money. Larger aircraft that have more seats not only haul more, they weigh more. That means it needs a bigger engine and more fuel to drag itself and all the pilot's stuff through the air.

A great example of the value of this type of aircraft is the Cessna 172. Cessna stopped production of the single-engine piston line (in fact all piston-engine aircraft) in 1986. When they decided to re-enter the market in 1997, they didn't start with big, six-place, retractable-gear aircraft that would make the most money on each sale. They didn't even look to the small-business market and produce a piston twin. What they brought back was the world-renowned 172. This four-place, fixed-gear, fixed-propeller simple aircraft was the first to be reproduced. Not only was there an interest in the aircraft as personal transportation, there was also a training market.

Sure, other manufacturers at the time were still producing new aircraft for the market, but nothing made news or helped the resurgence of general aviation more than the Cessna 172. And like the 172, most of the aircraft on this list are OK at most of the things pilots ask them to do, but none are really great. Many owners expect a four-seater to truly be a four-seat aircraft, which is not true in most cases. Many times the aircraft is really a "two-plus-two" type of arrangement. In other words, it might haul four average adults, but not four average adults *and* full tanks or four adults *and* a lot of baggage. Decisions have to be made as to what is most important on each trip.

At higher elevations especially, four-place aircraft become two-place aircraft. The larger horsepower engines provide the better takeoff and climb performance required at high altitudes, but the minute they're loaded down with the weight of more than two people, you can kiss that performance good-bye.

The advantages the four-place, fixed-gear aircraft are lower operational costs, improved cockpit comfort, and increased useful loads and cruise speeds. Most of these aircraft offer seats that are raised high enough to allow the pilot and passenger(s) to straighten their legs on long, cross-country flights. They also offer the shoulder and hip room to make the flight less cramped and more relaxed.

And if comfort isn't enough, cruise speeds can be anywhere from 130 miles per hour on up. Cross-country travel becomes a reality. Not that you can't take a smaller aircraft on long trips; I once delivered a Cessna 152 to New Orleans, Louisiana, from Iowa. It is a long flight, but it can be done. I also know a couple who took their 1962 Cessna 150 all the way to Mexico and back for a two-week vacation. The fuel cost was almost as cheap as driving *and* it was a lot more fun. So, as you can see, a four-place aircraft isn't always a requirement for longer trips, but they usually offer a little more room and comfort.

Of course, the more aircraft you have and the heavier the load it can carry, the bigger the engine has to be. And with bigger engines come more fuel consumption and larger fuel capacities. Of course, the more fuel the aircraft can carry, the longer the flight can be.

Because of their size and weight, four-seat aircraft are also usually a little smoother in rough air. Turbulence doesn't bounce them around as much as it does smaller aircraft. This also makes them great training platforms for advanced ratings like the instrument, for example, since the larger panels in four-place aircraft usually feature more instruments and gauges.

Whatever model fits the needs, it is always important to remember that a four-place, is not really a four-place… except on the perfect day.

Beechcraft Musketeer

The Beechcraft Musketeer has always been a little behind the marketplace. The Musketeer, Sport, and Sundowner all share the same trailing-link landing gear. This gear is well built and very durable, but its design restricts the addition of wheel fairings that the aircraft could use to pick up a few miles per hour in cruise.

Production of the Musketeer started in 1963 with a Lycoming 160-horsepower engine but changed to an odd Continental 165-horsepower engine (the IO346A) the following year. The Musketeer offers reasonable performance but the engine is in short supply and parts are becoming more and more difficult to locate. The 165 HP engine was used in the Musketeer 23 A from 1964 until 1968. Just over 1,000 of these aircraft were built.

The Beechcraft Musketeer and Sport lines are durable, basic aircraft. Most Musketeers, like this 1966 model, can be purchased very reasonably. They also offer lots of cockpit head- and legroom.

The Beechcraft Musketeer, Sport, and Sundowner are basically the same airplane with different engines and horsepower, as well as cosmetic improvements. A major component that never changed was the trailing-link landing gear renowned for durability and providing smooth landings.

Beechcraft Musketeer	
Cost of Operation	****
Cockpit Comfort	****
Cruise Speed	**
Useful Load	*
Serviceability and Parts Availability	***
Engine manufacturer and horsepower	Lycoming 160hp
Construction	Metal
Landing gear	Tri-gear
Maximum seating	4
Gross weight	2,300 lb

Beechcraft Musketeer—*continued*	
Useful load	1,000 lb
Cruise speed	111 mph
Stall speed	52 mph
Takeoff run	925 ft.
Takeoff run 50 feet	1,275 ft.
Landing roll	640 ft.
Standard fuel capacity	60 gal
Range	800 mi.
Fuel burn per hour	8 GPH
Last year of production	1970
Manufacturer in business?	Yes
Good availability?	No

The Beechcraft Sport was produced from 1966 through 1978 and was basically the same as the Musketeer but used a Lycoming 150-horsepower engine. *Photo courtesy of* Aero Trader

Beechcraft Sport

Built from 1966 to 1978, the Beechcraft Sport 19 is a version of the standard Musketeer but uses the Lycoming 150-horsepower engine. Though the aircraft still utilizes the trailing-link landing gear, it offers two doors and a cabin shape that provides a lot of cabin space, especially head- and legroom. Most of the Musketeer line is looked upon the same way we usually look at reliable old pickup trucks: they haul a decent cargo and are easy to load and unload. But they lack in cruise speed and don't like to rotate, making them long-runway aircraft. Over 90 Sport models were built in those 13 years.

Beechcraft Sport	
Cost of Operation	****
Cockpit Comfort	****
Cruise Speed	*
Useful Load	*
Serviceability and Parts Availability	***

Beechcraft Sport—*continued*	
Engine manufacturer and horsepower	Lycoming 150hp
Construction	Metal
Landing gear	Tri-gear
Maximum seating	4
Gross weight	2,150 lb
Useful load	736 lb
Cruise speed	107 mph
Stall speed	50 mph
Takeoff run	824 ft.
Takeoff run 50 feet	1,693 ft.
Landing roll	824 ft.
Standard fuel capacity	57 gal
Range	643 mi.
Fuel burn per hour	8 GPH
Last year of production	1978
Manufacturer in business?	Yes
Good availability?	No

The Beechcraft Sundowner, like the Musketeer and the Sport, has a roomy cockpit, trailing link landing gear, and two doors. The significant difference is that is uses a 180-horsepower Lycoming engine that generates better all-around performance. *Photo courtesy of* Aero Trader

Pilots tired of the fixed-gear Sundowner can always move up the Sierra, essentially a 200-horsepower Sundowner with retractable wheels.

The design of the Sierra's retractable gear is unique to the aircraft in that it lifts up and away from the center of the aircraft.

Beechcraft Sundowner	
Cost of Operation	****
Cockpit Comfort	****
Cruise Speed	***
Useful Load	*
Serviceability and Parts Availability	****
Engine manufacturer and horsepower	Lycoming 180hp
Construction	Metal
Landing gear	Tri-gear
Maximum seating	4
Gross weight	2,450 lb
Useful load	956 lb
Cruise speed	116 mph
Stall speed	51 mph
Takeoff run	1,130 ft.
Takeoff run 50 feet	1,955 ft.
Landing roll	703 ft.
Standard fuel capacity	57 gal
Range	565 mi.
Fuel burn per hour	10 GPH
Last year of production	1983
Manufacturer in business?	Yes
Good availability?	Yes

Beechcraft Sundowner

The Sundowner is an upgraded Musketeer. The addition of the Lycoming 180-horsepower engine changed the performance for the better, making the aircraft capable of respectable cruise speeds up to 134 miles per hour. The Sundowner is also stable in the air and affords plenty of room for headsets and passengers. Sundowners are capable trainers with gear systems that allow numerous hard landings with few problems. More than 1,200 Sundowners were built from 1968 to 1983.

Cessna 172 (Continental-powered)

Cessna designed the 172 line in 1956 as a replacement for their 170 model tailwheel aircraft. At the time, the trend toward tricycle-gear aircraft was in its infancy and designers reasoned that if handling an airplane felt more like driving a car, consumers would be more interested in the aircraft. In fact, the Cessna 172's landing gear was called "Land-o-Matic" in reference to the ease of flying it offered.

The first series of 172s used a six-cylinder Continental engine that produced 145 horsepower. The first models also had a straight tail and sloped tail cone that lasted until 1960, when the vertical fin was changed to the swept version, still with no back windows. In 1961, the name "Skyhawk" was added to

The Cessna 172 is one of the most popular single-engine aircraft ever produced and, after a brief hiatus, resumed production in 1997. The model year, 1956, featured a basic four-place cabin, 145-horsepower Continental engine, and a distinguishing straight tail. This post-1962 example has received the "Skyhawk" moniker (added in 1961) and "Omni-vision" rear windows (added in 1963). *Photo Courtesy of Cessna Aircraft Company*

upgraded versions. In 1963, Cessna added the "Omni-vision" rear windows, improving visibility but increasing gross weight by 50 pounds to 2,300.

Nineteen sixty four saw the last of the manual flaps, when electric switches were added to all new 172s. As with almost all aircraft, the 172 got bigger and heavier as the years passed. Logically, early models have the narrow cabins and least amount of noise protection.

Condition and hours are probably more important than year. And there's no shortage to choose from—more than 19,000 were built.

Cessna 172 (Continental-powered)	
Cost of Operation	****
Cockpit Comfort	***
Cruise Speed	**
Useful Load	*
Serviceability and Parts Availability	****
Engine manufacturer and horsepower	Continental 145hp
Construction	Metal
Landing gear	Tri-gear
Maximum seating	4
Gross weight	2,200 lb
Useful load	875 lb
Cruise speed	114 mph
Stall speed	51 mph
Takeoff run	875 ft.
Takeoff run 50 feet	1,370 ft.
Landing roll	600 ft.
Standard fuel capacity	42 gal
Range	515 mi.
Fuel burn per hour	8 GPH
Last year of production	1967
Manufacturer in business?	Yes
Good availability?	Yes

Cessna 172 (Lycoming-powered)

In 1968, the Cessna Skyhawk received the "Blue Streak" 150-horsepower Lycoming engine. This four-cylinder replaced the six-cylinder Continental while adding 5 horsepower and losing about 35 pounds. The Lycoming was also sold with a 2,000-hour time between overhaul (TBO) compared to the Continental's 1,800 TBO.

In 1969, long-range fuel capacity (52 gallons) was offered and, two years later, in 1971, Cessna added tubular-steel landing gear. As with the Cessna 150, this change lowered and widened the wheel tread of the aircraft, thereby improving the ground handling.

The 1977 model was the first with an AVCO Lycoming 160-horsepower engine. Designed as a replacement for the 150-horsepower, and manufactured to use the new 100 low-lead fuel being introduced at the time, the new powerplant was discovered to have a few internal problems, and numerous failures gave it a bad reputation. The dreaded "H2AD" engine forced Cessna to look for a replacement. The "D2J" was installed in 1981 to 1986 models. Because the H2AD has kept the resale values of 1977 to 1980 172N models down, buyers can find good opportunities with these models.

It should also be noted that the 1977 model is the last with a 12-volt electrical system. Not that it makes a big difference, but 12-volt batteries are cheaper and can be jump-started from a small battery cart or even an automobile. Also, 1980 is the last year with 40 degrees

From 1958 to 1962, Cessna produced a variation of the 172 that used a geared Continental engine. The 175 is distinguishable from the 172 by the ridge on the cowl behind the propeller to accommodate the propeller shaft's gear unit.

Cessna's switch to Lycoming for 172 power wasn't absolute. In 1979 they rolled out the Continental-powered 172 Hawk XP, the panel of which was the same as other 172s with the exception of a control for the constant-speed propeller.

In 1968, the Cessna 172 Skyhawk received a 150-horsepower Lycoming engine and, in 1971, was given tubular-steel landing gear. The 172 received several engine upgrades and tweaks through the end of production in 1986, the year this airplane was built. Cessna revived the model in 1997 with the 172R.

This did not come standard from the factory. The damage to the cone on this 1998 172R is the result of a windstorm, and should alert you to potential damage elsewhere. Once repaired, this aircraft was a great buy.

Cessna 172 (Lycoming-powered)	
Cost of Operation	*****
Cockpit Comfort	***
Cruise Speed	****
Useful Load	**
Serviceability and Parts Availability	*****
Engine manufacturer and horsepower	Lycoming 160hp
Construction	Metal
Landing gear	Tri-gear
Maximum seating	4
Gross weight	2,400 lb

Cessna 172 (Lycoming-powered)—*continued*	
Useful load	946 lb
Cruise speed	120 mph
Stall speed	46 mph
Takeoff run	890 ft.
Takeoff run 50 feet	1,625 ft.
Landing roll	540 ft.
Standard fuel capacity	43 gal
Optional fuel capacity	68 gal
Range	440 mi.
Fuel burn per hour	8 GPH
Last year of production	2001
Manufacturer in business?	Yes
Good availability?	Yes

of flap travel. From 1981 to 1986, the maximum flap travel available is 30 degrees.

More than 11,000 Skyhawks were built from 1968 to 1976, and just over 9,000 aircraft were produced from 1977 to the end of production in 1986. This doesn't include variations like the 180-horsepower fixed-gear Cutlass produced in 1983 and 1984, or the 172XP powered by a 195-horsepower Continental six-cylinder. Also, the aircraft went back into production in 1997, first with the introduction of the 172R that uses a de-rated engine producing 160 horsepower and then a model cranking out 180 horsepower. Both offer fuel injection and updated avionics.

Grumman American AA5

The American General line was expanded in 1972 to include a four-seat aircraft that offered the cruise performance of a small retractable without the headaches of retracts. The same bonded honeycomb construction used in the Yankee model was used in this enlarged version, as were the bubble canopy and castering nose wheel that gave it a sports-car feel. The early Traveler and Cheetah versions (1972 through 1979) were designated the AA5 and AA5A respectively. Both models use the Lycoming 150-horsepower engine and attain cruise speeds in the 138-mile-per-hour range, which is pretty impressive. But this cruise comes at a cost: the AA5 models are

The Grumman AA5 is essentially a four-seat version of the AA1 with the necessary horsepower upgrade; it was first produced in 1972 with a Lycoming 150 and through the years was offered with powerplants as large as the Lycoming 180. Like all AA5s, this 1975 model was manufactured using the same honeycomb-bonded method as the AA1, a technique that has been sporadically appropriated by other manufacturers.
Photo courtesy of LeRoy Cook

not the best for load hauling and short-field performance. Like their two-seat sibling, they like to use the runway.

In 1975, the AA5B was introduced as the Tiger, incorporating all the same features as the rest of the four-seat line but using a Lycoming 180-horsepower engine. This impressive aircraft has a book cruise speed of 160 miles per hour, an exceptional figure for a fixed-gear, fixed-propeller aircraft. In fact, the performance is as good as can be expected from some larger, more expensive aircraft. The problem is finding a good one. Only about 1,100 are still listed on the registry. About 1,120 AA5s and AA5As combined are listed.

But don't give up. The design has been moved around to a number of different owners and the Tiger is being re-introduced—of course at a substantially higher price. But if a well-maintained or restored Tiger shows up, it might be a good aircraft to look at.

Maule M-4

The Maule family has been hand-making aircraft from tube and fabric since the early 1960s. Since then, they have used numerous engines—both piston- and turbine-driven—built them with both tricycle gears and tailwheels, and put them on floats. The aircraft have a reputation as a bush plane but can be used as respectable cross-country cruisers. Their design and construction is pretty much the same today as in 1962, the only differences being in the avionics and options.

Through the years, Maule has produced both tri-gear and tail wheel versions of their aircraft. They have also incorporated various engines with horsepower ranging from 145 to a 420 Allison turboprop.

Grumman AA5	
Cost of Operation	*****
Cockpit Comfort	**
Cruise Speed	*****
Useful Load	*
Serviceability and Parts Availability	****
Engine manufacturer and horsepower	Lycoming 150hp
Construction	Metal
Landing gear	Tri-gear
Maximum seating	4
Gross weight	2,200 lb

Grumman AA5—*continued*	
Useful load	877 lb
Cruise speed	127 mph
Stall speed	52 mph
Takeoff run	880 ft.
Takeoff run 50 feet	1,600 ft.
Landing roll	1,100 ft.
Standard fuel capacity	37 gal
Optional fuel capacity	51 gal
Range	428 mi.
Fuel burn per hour	8 GPH
Last year of production	1993
Manufacturer in business?	Yes
Good availability?	Yes

One unique trait of the Maule M-4 is a three-door design that allows easier access to the rear seats, baggage compartment, and front seats. The feature is in part responsible for the Maule's reputation as a fine bush plane.

Maule M-4

Cost of Operation	***
Cockpit Comfort	***
Cruise Speed	*****
Useful Load	****
Serviceability and Parts Availability	****
Engine manufacturer and horsepower	Lycoming 180hp
Construction	Tube and fabric
Landing gear	Tri-gear
Maximum seating	4
Gross weight	2,400 lb
Useful load	1,050 lb
Cruise speed	140 mph
Stall speed	40 mph
Takeoff run	550 ft.
Takeoff run 50 feet	1,150 ft.
Landing roll	500 ft.
Standard fuel capacity	40 gal
Optional fuel capacity	70 gal
Range	500 mi.
Fuel burn per hour	10 GPH
Last year of production	2001
Manufacturer in business?	Yes
Good availability?	Yes

Modern Maule aircraft are known for especially well-equipped instrument panels.

This 1999 Piper Archer III is loaded with avionics, including a stormscope and three-axis autopilot. *Photo courtesy of Norm Goyer*

Piper Archer	
Cost of Operation	****
Cockpit Comfort	****
Cruise Speed	****
Useful Load	**
Serviceability and Parts Availability	*****
Engine manufacturer and horsepower	Lycoming 180hp
Construction	Metal
Landing gear	Tri-gear
Maximum seating	4
Gross weight	2,450 lb
Useful load	1,055 lb

Piper Archer—*continued*	
Cruise speed	123 mph
Stall speed	53 mph
Takeoff run	720 ft.
Takeoff run 50 feet	1,625 ft.
Landing roll	635 ft.
Standard fuel capacity	50 gal
Range	507 mi.
Fuel burn per hour	10 GPH
Last year of production	2001
Manufacturer in business?	Yes
Good availability?	Yes

The Archer III cowling is designed for efficiency and looks. The scoops increase the pressure of incoming air, providing better cooling and reducing drag. *Photo courtesy of John B. McLaughlin*

Piper Archer

The Piper Archer, or PA28-181, has been produced from 1976 until the present. Production has totaled more than 3,600 so far. They have proven excellent aircraft for training, weekend flying, and cross-country travel, with their 180-horsepower Lycoming engine providing an economical solution to the four-place dilemma. Also, the 181, like later Warriors, utilizes a tapered wing to provide improved handling and better cruise speeds.

The only factor adversely affecting the Archer is resale. A well-maintained or restored aircraft can fetch a substantial price. Times and conditions are still the key. An old, nice aircraft can bring higher prices than newer, rougher aircraft. And the models do not show much visible evidence between the old and the new.

Piper Cherokee 140

The Piper Cherokee 140 (PA28-140) was introduced in 1964 as a trainer replacement for the 150 and 160. Its original incarnation featured a short fuselage; a thick, short wing (nicknamed the "Hershey bar wing"); and no external baggage door. The aircraft could actually be licensed as a four-seater but the rear seat is a snap-in "jump seat" with a cushion and not much legroom. In the later years, some were even sold with air conditioning.

A 150-horsepower engine was the powerplant of choice and stayed in place until 1977. Many early models have manual flaps and manual parking brakes. Toe brakes were optional and not always installed on both sets of controls. It's not unusual to see a Cherokee owner reaching below the panel to pull the brake handle and slow the 140 to a stop. There were 10,089 Cherokees built before the model transitioned into the Warrior.

The Cherokee 140 was Piper's attempt to compete with the Cessna 150 trainer. The 140 offered a 150-horsepower Lycoming engine, two-plus-two seating, and tricycle gear. The wing was built with a constant cord, thick airfoil, and short span. The design earned the nickname "Hershey bar" wing as seen on this 1974 model.

Early Cherokees have short, constant-chord wings dubbed "Hershey bar" wings because of their shape.

One distinguishing characteristic of the entire Piper Cherokee line is the stabilator, a horizontal stabilizer and elevator (with trim tab) designed as one piece rather than separately as on other aircraft.

Piper Cherokee 140	
Cost of Operation	****
Cockpit Comfort	***
Cruise Speed	**
Useful Load	*
Serviceability and Parts Availability	****
Engine manufacturer and horsepower	Lycoming 150hp
Construction	Metal
Landing gear	Tri-gear
Maximum seating	4
Gross weight	2,150 lb
Useful load	860 lb
Cruise speed	110 mph
Stall speed	48 mph
Takeoff run	800 ft.
Takeoff run 50 feet	1,700 ft.
Landing roll	535 ft.
Standard fuel capacity	36 gal
Optional fuel capacity	50 gal
Range	455 mi.
Fuel burn per hour	8 GPH
Last year of production	1977
Manufacturer in business?	Yes
Good availability?	Yes

Piper Cherokee 150/160

Built from 1962 through 1967, the PA28-150 and PA28-160 Cherokees actually feature the same airframe as the PA28-180— longer with a small exterior baggage door, hat shelf, and permanent rear seats. The aircraft use Lycoming 150- and 160–horsepower engines, respectively, and incorporate the "Hershey bar" wings that are the Cherokee's trademark. Simple to maintain and easy to fly, the aircraft offer decent performance for their cost. They use manual flaps, manual brakes, and a fixed-pitch propeller. The 160 was available as a floatplane, but the 150 was not. Between the 150, 160, and 180, 7,422 Cherokees were built.

Piper Cherokee 180

Built from 1961 to 1975, the Piper Cherokee PA28-180 was probably one of the first almost-true, four-place aircraft. With the same short, thick wing as the other Cherokees, the 180 has a beefier 180-horsepower Lycoming engine. Finally, pilots could take a full load of people and still have room for fuel. The performance is good and, as a bonus, the aircraft is still simple, relying on manual flaps, a fixed-pitch propeller, and higher horsepower to make the numbers.

The 1974 model was the first Archer built, and its thick wing didn't change until the 1976 Archer II model.

Piper Cherokee 150 and 160	
Cost of Operation	***
Cockpit Comfort	****
Cruise Speed	*
Useful Load	**
Serviceability and Parts Availability	***
Engine manufacturer and horsepower	Lycoming 150/160hp
Construction	Metal
Landing gear	Tri-gear
Maximum seating	4
Gross weight	2,150 lb

Piper Cherokee 150 and 160—*continued*	
Useful load	945 lb
Cruise speed	107 mph
Stall speed	47 mph
Takeoff run	780 ft.
Takeoff run 50 feet	1,750 ft
Landing roll	535 ft.
Standard fuel capacity	36 gal
Optional fuel capacity	50 gal
Range	435 mi.
Fuel burn per hour	8 GPH
Last year of production	1967
Manufacturer in business?	Yes
Good availability?	No

The Cherokee 180 is an improved 140 with an exterior baggage door and 180-horsepower Lycoming engine. In addition, Cherokee 150s and 160s utilize the same airframe with smaller engines. Cherokee 150s, 160s, and 180s offer a true rear-seat compared to the 140's snap-in pads, which are really glorified jump seats. In 1968, five years after this example was built, Piper added a third window on each side.

Early Cherokees all had the same small spinner. But in 1968, the 180 was given a larger spinner to distinguish it from earlier and smaller models, to streamline its design, and to enhance its performance.

Piper Cherokee 180	
Cost of Operation	***
Cockpit Comfort	****
Cruise Speed	****
Useful Load	****
Serviceability and Parts Availability	****
Engine manufacturer and horsepower	Lycoming 180hp
Construction	Metal
Landing gear	Tri-gear
Maximum seating	4
Gross weight	2,400 lb
Useful load	1,170 lb
Cruise speed	124 mph
Stall speed	50 mph
Takeoff run	720 ft.
Takeoff run 50 feet	1,620 ft.
Landing roll	600 ft.
Standard fuel capacity	50 gal
Range	510 mi.
Fuel burn per hour	10 GPH
Last year of production	1975
Manufacturer in business?	Yes
Good availability?	Yes

The Piper Tri-Pacer was produced from 1951 through 1960. The four-place, tube and-fabric, tricycle-gear aircraft was built with a 125- to 160-horsepower Lycoming engine. From 1961 through 1963, the aircraft was also produced as the PA22-108 or Piper Colt. This is a 150-horsepower equipped 1956 model.

From 1950 to 1954, Piper produced a tailwheeled Tri-Pacer dubbed simply, the Pacer. Many Tri-Pacers have been converted to tail wheel aircraft by their diehard, tail-dragging owners. The diminutive wingspan of both the Tri-Pacer and Pacer has earned the aircraft the appellation "Short Wing Pipers."

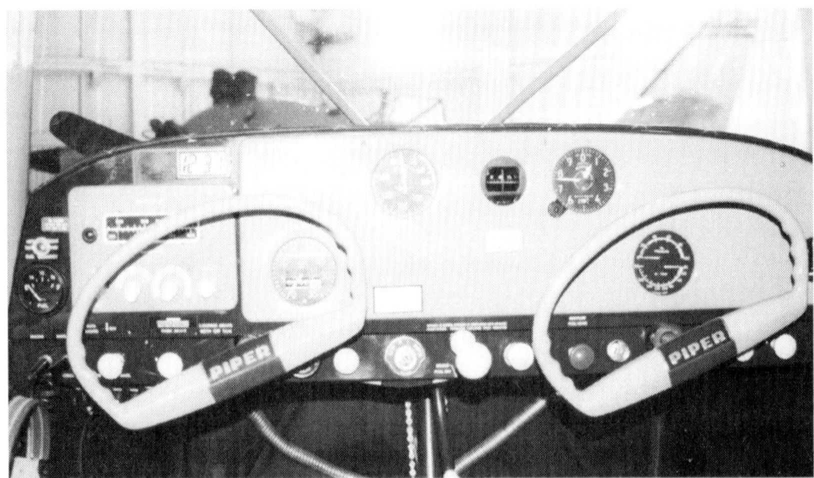

In the 1950s, the Tri-Pacer offered all the conveniences of modern navigation, which at the time was one step above dead reckoning.

Most Tri-Pacers still in service have had their panels reconfigured to include more avionics and instruments.

Tri-Pacers have a unique elevator trim system that moves the horizontal stabilizer at its leading edge.

Piper Tri-Pacer

The PA22-135/150/160 represents Piper's entry into the four-place, tricycle-gear market. For a few years beginning in 1951, it was built alongside the Pacer, a tailwheel version. Many later Tri-Pacers have, in fact, been converted to the Pacer style by diehard tail-draggers.

Produced until 1963, more than 9,400 aircraft rolled off the line, featuring engines that ranged from 135 to 160 horsepower. This tube-and-fabric tricycle design was nicknamed the "flying milk stool" for the way its landing gear looks, the mains and nose mounted close together and sitting high. The Tri-Pacer is also a member of the "short wing" Piper club, a group that features short wing spans and a moderate sink rate when power is reduced or at idle.

The Tri-Pacer is not a difficult aircraft to fly but it has been noted to land hard and to tip over (like a milk stool) if the pilot tries to turn too sharp while going too fast. And while tube and-fabric aircraft require a little different care than all-metal aircraft, some Tri-Pacers have been metalized, adding weight and reducing performance. *And* this modification still doesn't stop the risk of corrosion of the tubing. A few specific concerns about the wing struts should also be considered when your mechanic inspects the aircraft. The wing struts were found to get moisture inside and develop corrosion.

Piper Tri-Pacer	
Cost of Operation	***
Cockpit Comfort	****
Cruise Speed	****
Useful Load	*
Serviceability and Parts Availability	***
Engine manufacturer and horsepower	Lycoming 150hp
Construction	Tube and fabric
Landing gear	Tri-gear
Maximum seating	4
Gross weight	1,950 lb
Useful load	890 lb
Cruise speed	122 mph
Stall speed	49 mph
Takeoff run	1,120 ft.
Takeoff run 50 feet	1,600 ft.
Landing roll	1,280 ft.
Standard fuel capacity	36 gal
Optional fuel capacity	44 gal
Range	430 mi.
Fuel burn per hour	8 GPH
Last year of production	1963
Manufacturer in business?	Yes
Good availability?	Yes

Piper Warrior

Piper Warrior (PA28-151 and 161) production began in 1974 and continues until the present. The Warrior incorporates significant changes from the Cherokee 140. Most noticeably, the wings were changed to a thinner, tapered airfoil. In addition, handling is reportedly better, but increases in cabin size and useful load also decrease the book cruise performance. The production of the 151 has thus far totaled 1,898.

The 161 features a 160-horsepower engine and surpasses the 140 and 151 in cruise speed. The power quadrant is the standard configuration for the throttle and mixture controls, giving the Warrior a large aircraft feel. Records indicate that more than 3,300 PA28-161 Warrior IIs and IIIs have been built from 1977 to the present.

In 1974, Piper modified and tapered the short, stubby wing of the Cherokee 140, and upgraded the engine. The result was this airplane, named the "Warrior." While the Warrior retains the Cherokee look, it offers improved performance and handling. In 1977, Piper began offering the PA28-161, named the Warrior II and using a 160-horsepower Lycoming. Factory specs indicated a cruise speed of 127 knots compared to 109 in the 150-horsepower Warrior.

The typical Warrior panel offers IFR capabilities and a standard layout consistent with the Cherokee line.

The TB-10 is a 200-horsepower TB-9—the same airframe with more horsepower and a higher useful load.

Piper Warrior	
Cost of Operation	*****
Cockpit Comfort	****
Cruise Speed	***
Useful Load	**
Serviceability and Parts Availability	*****
Engine manufacturer and horsepower	Lycoming 160hp
Construction	Metal
Landing gear	Tri-gear
Maximum seating	4
Gross weight	2,325 lb
Useful load	981 lb
Cruise speed	118 mph
Stall speed	44 mph
Takeoff run	975 ft.
Takeoff run 50 feet	1,650 ft.
Landing roll	595 ft.
Standard fuel capacity	48 gal
Range	525 mi.
Fuel burn per hour	8 GPH
Last year of production	2001
Manufacturer in business?	Yes
Good availability?	Yes

Socata TB-9 Tampico and TB-10 Tobago

The Tampico and Tobago are almost identical in appearance and style. The major difference is the options and horsepower of the engines. The Tampico is produced as a trainer with Lycoming's 160–horsepower engine. This provides a respectable cruise speed and economical operational cost for the flight schools. Both aircraft use gull-wing doors and sports-car styling in the cockpit, helping make the Socata line of aircraft popular.

The Tobago uses a 180-horsepower Lycoming. A few models are available as the TB200XL with a 200-horsepower engine. The TB-10 was the first entry into the trainer market, being introduced in 1986 and still selling today. The TB-9 was released in 1990 and has remained in production since that time.

Transition between the TB-10 and the TB-9, or even the high-performance TB-21, is very easy. Besides a little bigger airframe, the pilot feels right at home in any of the models.

Automotive styling, digital electronics, and a "custom feel" are common to the control panels of all Socata aircraft.

Socata TB-9 Tampico	
Cost of Operation	*****
Cockpit Comfort	****
Cruise Speed	*
Useful Load	*
Serviceability and Parts Availability	****
Engine manufacturer and horsepower	Lycoming 160hp
Construction	Metal
Landing gear	Tri-gear
Maximum seating	4
Gross weight	2,337 lb
Useful load	926 lb
Cruise speed	106 mph
Stall speed	50 mph
Takeoff run	1,066 ft.
Takeoff run 50 feet	1,706 ft.
Landing roll	623 ft.
Standard fuel capacity	42 gal
Range	500 mi.
Fuel burn per hour	8 GPH
Last year of production	2001
Manufacturer in business?	Yes
Good availability?	No

Socata TB-10 Tobago	
Cost of Operation	****
Cockpit Comfort	****
Cruise Speed	***
Useful Load	*
Serviceability and Parts Availability	****
Engine manufacturer and horsepower	Lycoming 180hp
Construction	Metal
Landing gear	Tri-gear
Maximum seating	4
Gross weight	2,535 lb
Useful load	1,058 lb
Cruise speed	117 mph
Stall speed	51 mph
Takeoff run	1,066 ft.
Takeoff run 50 feet	1,657 ft.
Landing roll	623 ft.
Standard fuel capacity	54 gal
Range	425 mi.
Fuel burn per hour	10 GPH
Last year of production	2001
Manufacturer in business?	Yes
Good availability?	No

Chapter 6

Four- and Six-Seat High-Performance Complex Aircraft

There are always a few among us who want to fly faster, carry more, or go farther than anyone else. For those looking for more, there are a number of good aircraft that might meet their needs.

Most manufacturers have produced a few models that are unique in design or purpose and offer a few things the others can't. These aircraft are not always the easiest to fly and they definitely increase insurance and operational cost—not because they're inferior but because they are more complex to operate and maintain. They have larger airframes and engines and burn more fuel, and have higher overhaul costs. They are also more apt to be used in commercial operations, which often times makes them more desirable on the used market, driving prices up and availability down.

But sometimes a few aircraft do offer more than expected. The Cessna 205 and 206 and the Piper Cherokee Six models are prime examples. To paraphrase a line from a Cessna advertisement, they are "Aviation's versions of sport-utility vehicles." These aircraft offer the load-hauling capabilities and the seating and headroom that many people are looking for. They are desirable in the back country and on mission trips because they can carry ample supplies and cargo. They are also big enough to accommodate stretchers and even to sleep in!

Whatever the aircraft need, there is something for everyone, even on the small list that follows. Some of the aircraft included here are among the most popular and are readily available on the used market. Of these, the Cessna 205 is one of the harder to find. But it can be done.

Cessna 172RG

The Cessna 172RG Cutlass was a very good complex training aircraft. Designed with the reliable Lycoming 180-horsepower engine and a constant-speed, two-bladed propeller, it also features landing gear that are reliable but which have, nonetheless, garnered a few airworthiness directives (Ads)and service bulletins that can add to maintenance costs.

The worst thing about the aircraft, however, is that even with wheels that fold up and streamline the aircraft, its increase in cruise speed is not spectacular. The factory books indicate it will fly about 161 miles

From 1980 to 1985, Cessna offered the 172RG, which used a 180-horsepower engine, constant-speed propeller, and retractable landing gear. The 172RG was extremely popular as a complex trainer. *Photo courtesy of LeRoy Cook*

per hour but, realistically, 150 miles per hour is more likely. Still, the cruise is better than the standard 172 and comparable to the fixed-gear Cessna 182. Although the 172RG won't haul as much as the 182, its advantageous in the fact that it burns less fuel and is cheaper to maintain, even with retractable gear.

Of the 1,191 172RGs Cessna built from 1980 to 1985, the aircraft to be careful of are high-time, poorly maintained, former trainers. Hard landings and repetitive cycling of the gear can put a lot of wear and tear on the gear system. When properly maintained and flown, it can be a very good cross-country cruiser.

Cessna 172RG	
Cost of Operation	*****
Cockpit Comfort	***
Cruise Speed	**
Useful Load	*
Serviceability and Parts Availability	***
Engine manufacturer and horsepower	Lycoming 180hp
Construction	Metal
Landing gear	Retractable
Maximum seating	4
Gross weight	2,650 lb
Useful load	1,023 lb
Cruise speed	140 mph
Stall speed	50 mph
Takeoff run	1,060 ft.
Takeoff run 50 feet	1,775 ft.
Landing roll	625 ft.
Standard fuel capacity	66 gal
Range	720 mi.
Fuel burn per hour	10 GPH
Last year of production	1985
Manufacturer in business?	Yes
Good availability?	No

Cessna 177 Cardinal

The first year of the ultramodern Cardinal was 1968. This aircraft was a completely new design for Cessna. The fully cantilevered wing has a large spar through the cabin but no struts. The doors are huge, almost 4 feet across, and open to 90 degrees, also with no struts! In addition, wing location and sweptback windshield increase forward visibility. Negative design elements include cockpit entry through big doors, which makes the aircraft very easy to overload.

The 1968 model uses a 150-horsepower engine that makes the aircraft seem underpowered. The high-performance laminar flow-wing produces great handling and cruise speed, but at the expense of prolonged takeoff runs. And the Cardinal uses a stabilator instead of a fixed horizontal stabilizer and elevator. The stabilator actually offered more control

The 177 Cardinal was Cessna's attempt to modernize and replace the 172. The 177 uses a full-cantilever, laminar-flow wing that eliminates the need for external struts. This is an example of the model's first year, 1968. The inaugural year's Lycoming 150-horsepower engine turned out to be an underperformer, so the following year, Cessna replaced it with a 180. To improve cruise and climb performance, a constant-speed propeller became standard in 1970.

The 177's panel is similar to that of the 172 and often includes controls for an autopilot feature.

The 1968 177's horizontal stabilator provided more control than the underpowered plane could handle.

In 1971, Cessna increased the performance of the 177 by installing a 200-horsepower Lycoming engine and adding retractable landing gear. The resulting 177RG achieves cruise speeds up to 184 knots. *Photo courtesy of LeRoy Cook*

than the underpowered, overloaded plane (or pilots) could handle, a condition that prompted insurance companies to dislike the 1968 model unless it was converted to a bigger engine and had slots installed in the stabilator. The slots kept air flowing over the stabilator offering improved control, and prevented the tail from stalling.

In 1969, the Cardinal was upgraded to the Lycoming 180-horsepower engine and a fixed-pitch propeller, a great combination for performance and operating costs. In 1970, Cessna added a constant-speed propeller to the mix and increased the performance even more, but at the expense of increased cost. Additionally, the airfoil was changed in 1970 to help lower the stalling speed, thereby improving slow -speed handling. This combination lasted for the remainder of the production run, which ended in 1978. More than 2,750 aircraft were produced.

Cessna 177 Cardinal (Lycoming 150)	
Cost of Operation	****
Cockpit Comfort	*****
Cruise Speed	***
Useful Load	*
Serviceability and Parts Availability	***
Engine manufacturer and horsepower	Lycoming 150hp
Construction	Metal
Landing gear	Tri-gear
Maximum seating	4
Gross weight	2,350 lb
Useful load	935 lb
Cruise speed	117 mph
Stall speed	46 mph
Takeoff run	845 ft.
Takeoff run 50 feet	1,575 ft.
Landing roll	400 ft.
Standard fuel capacity	49 gal
Range	591 mi.
Fuel burn per hour	8 GPH
Last year of production	1968
Manufacturer in business?	Yes
Good availability?	No

Cessna 177 Cardinal (Lycoming 180)	
Cost of Operation	***
Cockpit Comfort	*****
Cruise Speed	****
Useful Load	***
Serviceability and Parts Availability	****
Engine manufacturer and horsepower	Lycoming 180hp
Construction	Metal
Landing gear	Tri-gear
Maximum seating	4
Gross weight	2,500 lb
Useful load	1,060 lb
Cruise speed	120 mph
Stall speed	49 mph
Takeoff run	845 ft.
Takeoff run 50 feet	1,220 ft.
Landing roll	435 ft.
Standard fuel capacity	49 gal
Range	410 mi.
Fuel burn per hour	10 GPH
Last year of production	1978
Manufacturer in business?	Yes
Good availability?	Yes

Cessna 177RG	
Cost of Operation	****
Cockpit Comfort	*****
Cruise Speed	**
Useful Load	****
Serviceability and Parts Availability	****
Engine manufacturer and horsepower	Lycoming 200hp
Construction	Metal
Landing gear	Retractable
Maximum seating	4
Gross weight	2,800 lb
Useful load	1,170 lb
Cruise speed	144 mph
Stall speed	50 mph
Takeoff run	890 ft.
Takeoff run 50 feet	1,585 ft.
Landing roll	730 ft.
Standard fuel capacity	51 gal
Range	506 mi.
Fuel burn per hour	10 GPH
Last year of production	1978
Manufacturer in business?	Yes
Good availability?	No

Cessna 177RG

In 1971, Cessna decided to make the Cardinal faster by retracting the wheels with a system similar to that used on the 210 model. They also installed a 200-horsepower Lycoming engine that helped the 177RG generate a cruise of more than 170 miles per hour.

The aircraft is quite a performer in the air, but it still has a high-performance wing that requires lots of runway and air speed to keep it flying. Additionally, the landing gear generates a number of problems and has caused numerous gear-up landings throughout the aircraft's history. It's not unusual to find a 177RG with gear-up damage—just make sure it's been repaired correctly and that the aircraft has been maintained. Only 1,366 177RGs were built from 1971 to 1978.

Cessna 180

The Cessna 180 Skywagon is, as its name suggests, a station wagon for the back-country pilot. Powered by Continental's reliable 230-horsepower engine, the Skywagon is essentially a tailwheel version of the Cessna 182. The 180 was produced in large numbers from 1953 until 1981 (though the Skywagon moniker wasn't bestowed on it until 1969), and has seen use all over the world as a mission plane, family hauler, and floatplane. The aircraft started as a four-seat aircraft but with a gross-weight increase and cabin change was converted to a six-seater in 1964. It remained a six-seat aircraft (although the back two seats are quite small) for the remainder of its production run.

Many Skywagons have had floats or STOL (Short Take Off and Landing) kits installed to make their short-field performance even better. But the 180, like many

The Cessna 180 was produced as a tailwheel aircraft from 1953 to 1981. Until 1963, it was a 230-horsepower, four-place aircraft; from 1964 to the end of its production it was classified as a six-place airplane. Due to their solid construction and exceptional short-field performance, both the 180 and 185 are often sought after for use as bushplanes and floatplanes.

Cessna 180	
Cost of Operation	**
Cockpit Comfort	****
Cruise Speed	*****
Useful Load	***
Serviceability and Parts Availability	****
Engine manufacturer and horsepower	Continental 230hp
Construction	Metal
Landing gear	Tailwheel
Maximum seating	6
Gross weight	2,650 lb
Useful load	1,095 lb
Cruise speed	139 mph
Stall speed	54 mph
Takeoff run	615 ft.
Takeoff run 50 feet	1,080 ft.
Landing roll	460 ft.
Standard fuel capacity	55 gal
Range	513 mi.
Fuel burn per hour	12 GPH
Last year of production	1981
Manufacturer in business?	Yes
Good availability?	Yes

Cessna models, is considered to have very good short-field capabilities even without a STOL kit. The 180 is also one of the only Cessna models that has maintained the straight vertical fin instead of the updated swept look.

Cessna 182 Skylane

The Cessna 182 entered production in 1956, stopped in 1986, and came back into production in 1997. The 182 is still considered one of the best all-around, four-place aircraft to own. It offers a well-balanced control feel and is a stable instrument flight rules (IFR) platform. It is also one of those aircraft that really can carry four passengers and still have room for fuel and a few bags on an overnight trip. The 182 does, however, have a tendency to be heavier on the pitch controls and to require a strong arm to maintain a nose-high attitude when landing. Many insurance claims are for nose gear and firewall damage, the results of hard landings.

The 182's 230-horsepower Continental engine burns about 14 gallons per hour and provides cruise speeds in the 150-to 160-mile-per-hour range. Not bad for an affordable four-place. Keep in mind, though, the first four production years have straight tails, narrow spring-steel landing gears, and narrow cockpits, the latter of which translates to less cabin room but faster speeds.

The "Skylane" name was introduced in 1958 as a designation for deluxe models. In 1960, the Skylane was given a swept vertical fin like many other Cessna

After resuming production in 1997, the Cessna 182 has again become a dominant, true four-place aircraft, continuing to provide solid cross-country capabilities with its 230-horsepower engine and constant-speed propeller. Even the early models with straight tails and narrow cabins provided more room and speed for the dollar than their competition. *Photo courtesy of Cessna Aircraft Company*

models, and in 1962 the flaps were changed from manual to electric. The 1962 model was also the first to feature "Omni-view" windows.

Bladder fuel tanks (tanks with rubber liners) are housed in the wings up through the 1978 models. Some pilots believe that the bladder tanks are more of a headache and prone to developing leaks and wrinkles, while others feel they are the best option for an aircraft that is often heavily stressed by the requirement to take off and land on floats, skis, and unpaved runways. Reportedly, such stressful conditions can loosen the rivets and seams in "wet wing" tanks and cause leaks.

In 1997, the Skylane was re-introduced with Lycoming's 235-horsepower engine. This combination requires a longer cowl that makes the nose gear appear to be mounted farther back. The design was the same used earlier on approximately 60 Turbo Skylanes that Cessna produced from 1981 to 1986. In all, more than 19,000 182s were built, not including the turbo versions or models built from 1997 to the present.

Cessna R182

Speed is always on the aircraft designer's mind. How can an existing aircraft be made to go faster? If you can't

Two ways to help identify Cessna airplanes is by looking at their tails and rear windows. The squared top and straight, vertical fin and rudder, and lack of a rear window on this 182 are hallmarks of models produced from 1956 to 1959.

Beginning in 1960, Cessna gave the 182 a swept, vertical tail. The rear window on this example, however, helps give it away as a 1962 model, the first year of the "Omni-vision" feature. It was the same year that Cessna widened the cabin by 4 inches and replaced the manual flaps with electrically operated versions.

The Cessna 182 supports a large after market for owners looking to enhance their factory aircraft with optional equipment. STOL kits, three-bladed propellers, and long-range fuel tanks are some of the most popular modifications.

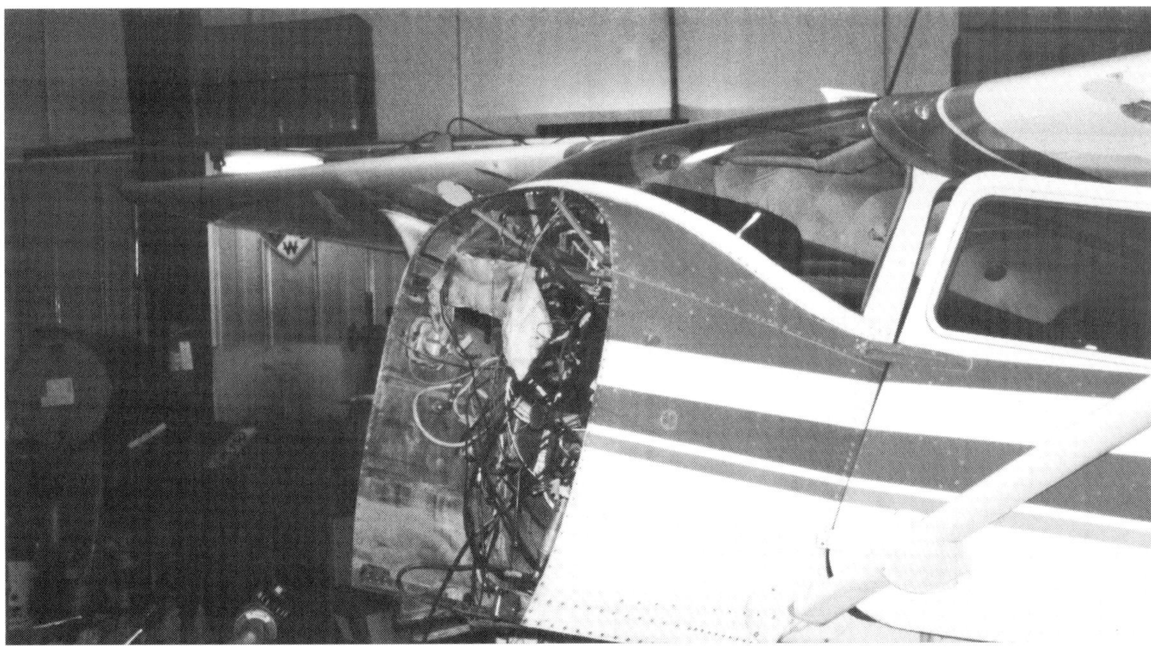

The 182 has a higher incidence of nose gear damage when the aircraft is lightly loaded but full of fuel. Nose gear impacts can cause firewall damage difficult for the non-mechanic to recognize. Such damage can require a complete replacement of the firewall.

Cessna 182 Skylane	
Cost of Operation	***
Cockpit Comfort	*****
Cruise Speed	*****
Useful Load	**
Serviceability and Parts Availability	*****
Engine manufacturer and horsepower	Continental 230hp
Construction	Metal
Landing gear	Tri-gear
Maximum seating	4
Gross weight	2,550 lb

Cessna 182 Skylane—*continued*	
Useful load	1,010 lb
Cruise speed	135 mph
Stall speed	54 mph
Takeoff run	620 ft.
Takeoff run 50 feet	1,020 ft.
Landing roll	610 ft.
Standard fuel capacity	55 gal
Range	443 mi.
Fuel burn per hour	12 GPH
Last year of production	2001
Manufacturer in business?	Yes
Good availability?	Yes

change the engine, retract the wheels. And that's just what designers did with the proven Cessna 182 Skylane. By taking their proven retract system and installing it on the 182, itself a proven performer, Cessna engineers increased the airplane's cruise speed to about 180 miles per hour without changing the fuel burn. The economic benefits are amazing: speed, comfort, and economy. You can't get much better than that!

Except maybe with the turbocharged version. The TR182, with a cruise speed of nearly 198 miles per hour, was built from 1979 to 1986. In fact, 1978 was the only year that the 182RG was manufactured without the turbo option. In addition, 1978 was also the last year of the bladder fuel tanks. In 1979, the R182 was fitted with wet wings and updated with the electric-hydraulic Powerpac system, making the retractable gears even more reliable.

In a quest to increase performance, Cessna modified its proven hydraulic, retractable landing gear for the R182. With a 235-horsepower engine and the reduced drag afforded by the retractable gear, R182s like this 1979 model are capable of cruise speeds over 156 knots.

The nose and cowling of the R182 were lengthened 15 1/2 inches to accommodate the Lycoming 230-horsepower engine and the retracting nose wheel. The airframe is known by mechanics for its lack of airworthiness directives (ADs). From 1979 to 1986, Cessna offered a turbocharged version of the airplane.

Cessna 182RG	
Cost of Operation	*****
Cockpit Comfort	*****
Cruise Speed	*****
Useful Load	**
Serviceability and Parts Availability	****
Engine manufacturer and horsepower	Lycoming 235hp
Construction	Metal
Landing gear	Retractable
Maximum seating	4
Gross weight	3,100 lb
Useful load	1,254 lb
Cruise speed	173 mph
Stall speed	50 mph
Takeoff run	820 ft.
Takeoff run 50 feet	1,570ft.
Landing roll	600 ft.
Standard fuel capacity	92 gal
Range	845 mi.
Fuel burn per hour	12 GPH
Last year of production	1986
Manufacturer in business?	Yes
Good availability?	Yes

The Cessna 185 is a great example of a popular bushplane. Beginning in 1961, the 185 was produced as a six-place, 260-horsepower aircraft. In 1966, it received a 300-horsepower upgrade that remained standard until 1985, the last production year. *Photo courtesy of LeRoy Cook*

Cessna 185

The Cessna 185 is the larger horsepower version of the 180. With a straight tail and tailwheel configuration it was, and still is, a desirable backcountry bush plane. The first models from 1961 to 1966 feature a Continental 260-horsepower engine. In 1967, Cessna changed to the 300-horsepower powerplant and increased the 185's gross weight, making it a pack mule of the skies. The 300-horsepower 185 was built until 1985.

To fill a need for more passenger space, Cessna stretched the 182 into a six-passenger airplane equipped with a 260-horsepower engine. The 205 was built in 1963 and 1964 and offered two front doors for the pilots and a rear door large enough for passengers and cargo. The 205 has a useful load of 1,550 pounds. *Photo courtesy of Cessna Aircraft Company*

Cessna 185	
Cost of Operation	**
Cockpit Comfort	****
Cruise Speed	***
Useful Load	**
Serviceability and Parts Availability	****
Engine manufacturer and horsepower	Continental 300hp
Construction	Metal
Landing gear	Tail wheel
Maximum seating	6
Gross weight	3,350 lb
Useful load	1,600 lb
Cruise speed	145 mph
Stall speed	49 mph
Takeoff run	825 ft.
Takeoff run 50 feet	1,430 ft.
Landing roll	610 ft.
Standard fuel capacity	88 gal
Range	645 mi.
Fuel burn per hour	16 GPH
Last year of production	1985
Manufacturer in business?	Yes
Good availability?	Yes

The aircraft has been used on floats, on skis, and as a crop-duster with a chemical hopper mounted on its belly. Cargo pods are used to increase useful loads, and six seats provided reasonable comfort on most flights. In 1978, the 185 was updated to a 24-volt electrical system, and in 1979 fuel bladders were eliminated and the wet-wing design incorporated. Not surprisingly, 4,400 of the aircraft were produced during its 24-year production run.

Cessna 205

If the 185 is a "country" plane, the 205 is Cessna's successful attempt at making a civilized six-place load hauler. The 205 is really a stretched version of the 182, featuring crew and passenger doors as well as a large cargo door. Increased cabin space allows a pilot to carry large items and offers excellent headroom for backseat passengers. The 205 is powered by the 260-horsepower Continental that is standard in the 185 and other twin-engine Cessnas. Cruise speed is a modest 160 miles per hour and useful load is around 1,550 pounds.

Cessna 205	
Cost of Operation	***
Cockpit Comfort	****
Cruise Speed	*
Useful Load	***
Serviceability and Parts Availability	***
Engine manufacturer and horsepower	Continental 260hp
Construction	Metal
Landing gear	Tri-gear
Maximum seating	6
Gross weight	3,300 lb

Cessna 205 *—continued*	
Useful load	1,550 lb
Cruise speed	138 mph
Stall speed	50 mph
Takeoff run	685 ft.
Takeoff run 50 feet	1,465 ft.
Landing roll	625 ft.
Standard fuel capacity	65 gal
Optional fuel capacity	84 gal
Range	515 mi.
Fuel burn per hour	14 GPH
Last year of production	1964
Manufacturer in business?	Yes
Good availability?	No

When the 206 was introduced in 1964, it was called the "Super Skywagon." Essentially a beefed-up 205 with heavy-duty rivet construction, a 285-horsepower engine, and improved brakes, the 206 has just one door on the pilot's side but large double doors on the passenger side. *Photo courtesy of Cessna Aircraft Company*

The 42-inch double doors make it easy to load all types of cargo into the 206. From 1965 to 1970, Cessna produced the Super Skylane, which is really a 206 without the cargo doors. *Photo courtesy of Cessna Aircraft Company*

A McCauley three-bladed prop now comes standard on the 206.

Cessna 206

Cessna's 206 is an upgrade of the 205. Several variants were produced from 1964 to 1986, and after a short break, the 206 and Turbo 206 were reintroduced to the aviation community in 1998. The most popular types are the "utility" versions designed with a door on the right side of the cockpit and a large cargo door on the left side of the passenger area. This two-piece cargo door allows the user to load the aircraft with everything from passengers to caskets.

Several 206s were shipped overseas for use as missionary and work planes in underdeveloped countries, which may account for the fact that more than 7,600 aircraft were built but less than half are still listed on the FAA registry. The 206s built from 1964 to 1966 used the Continental 285-horsepower engine. The turbo models continued with the 285-horsepower version until 1977, when Cessna increased horsepower

The panel of this 2000 model-year Cessna 206 is replete with state-of-the-art avionics.

to 310. For their part, the straight 206s saw an increase to 300 horsepower from 1967 to the end of production in 1986. The new models currently produced feature a Lycoming 310-horsepower engine.

Surprisingly, the 206 was never designed with club or face-to-face seating; they were always produced "airline" or "bus style" with all seats facing forward.

Cessna 206	
Cost of Operation	****
Cockpit Comfort	*****
Cruise Speed	**
Useful Load	*****
Serviceability and Parts Availability	*****
Engine manufacturer and horsepower	Continental 285hp
Construction	Metal
Landing gear	Tri-gear
Maximum seating	6
Gross weight	3,600 lb
Useful load	1,805 lb
Cruise speed	142 mph
Stall speed	53 mph
Takeoff run	910 ft.
Takeoff run 50 feet	1,810 ft.
Landing roll	735 ft.
Standard fuel capacity	65 gal
Optional fuel capacity	84 gal
Range	555 mi.
Fuel burn per hour	16 GPH
Last year of production	2001
Manufacturer in business?	Yes
Good availability?	Yes

Mooney M20s are best distinguished by their forward-swept tails. They are also known for their efficient operation and excellent performance: very few airplanes can obtain 180 miles per hour on a 180-horsepower engine and burn just 10 gallons per hour. However, this performance comes at the expense of cabin space. This M20 is from the 1964 production year.

Mooney also built a turbocharged and pressurized version of the M20—in very limited numbers. Just 32 M22 Mustangs were produced from 1966 to 1970.

Despite their smaller cabin size, most Mooneys are fully equipped for cross-country travel.

Mooney M20

If I were looking for the analytical pilot's aircraft, the Mooney would be it. The M20 series offers a short, compact fuselage with high-performance wings and retractable landing gear. And the Mooney produces the numbers that the analytical mind looks for.

The M20 with its 180-horsepower Lycoming can squeak out about 180 miles per hour cruise speed. That's 1 mile per hour per horsepower. Very efficient. But efficiency comes at a cost—the cabin is small, really a two-place aircraft with room for a small amount of baggage. Speed and economy are what this plane is about.

With its sports-car handling and solid construction, the Mooney more than makes up for its lack of cabin space. The cabin area is built with a welded tube structure to which the skin attaches. And Mooneys are built mostly with screws and not many rivets. While mechanics complain that this makes repairs time-consuming, owners brag about push-pull tubes, a lack of cables, a manual landing gear option, and performance. Mooney pilots are always talking about high performance and low operating costs—this is one time that speed doesn't cost as much as you might expect.

Mooney M20 (Lycoming 180)	
Cost of Operation	****
Cockpit Comfort	**
Cruise Speed	****
Useful Load	**
Serviceability and Parts Availability	****
Engine manufacturer and horsepower	Lycoming 180hp
Construction	Metal
Landing gear	Retractable
Maximum seating	4
Gross weight	2,575 lb
Useful load	1,050 lb
Cruise speed	150 mph
Stall speed	50 mph
Takeoff run	815 ft.
Takeoff run 50 feet	1,395 ft.
Landing roll	595 ft.
Standard fuel capacity	52 gal
Range	659 mi.
Fuel burn per hour	10 GPH
Last year of production	1978
Manufacturer in business?	Yes
Good availability?	Yes

Mooney M20 (Lycoming 200)	
Cost of Operation	****
Cockpit Comfort	**
Cruise Speed	*****
Useful Load	*
Serviceability and Parts Availability	****
Engine manufacturer and horsepower	Lycoming 200hp
Construction	Metal
Landing gear	Retractable
Maximum seating	4
Gross weight	2,575 lb
Useful load	975 lb
Cruise speed	160 mph
Stall speed	50 mph
Takeoff run	760 ft.
Takeoff run 50 feet	1,550 ft.
Landing roll	595 ft.
Standard fuel capacity	52 gal
Range	601 mi.
Fuel burn per hour	10 GPH
Last year of production	1977
Manufacturer in business?	Yes
Good availability?	Yes

But there are a few drawbacks. Insurance companies consider Mooneys high-performance aircraft. With its low stance on the ground, the aircraft isn't designed for operation on rough or turf strips. It also takes a lot of runway. All minor things if you want a good cross-country aircraft for two—and neither of you are more than about 5-foot-10 in height. If you are, start looking for the later model long-body Mooneys. You might be unhappy with the shorter one.

Early Mooneys were built with wood wings and tails. Unless you are a craftsman, you don't care about buying insurance, and you want to work on the aircraft yourself, you are better off staying away from

The 180-horsepower Piper Arrow was manufactured from 1967 to 1971. Both the 180 and the larger 200 offer the pilot a simple transition to a more complex aircraft.

the wood. Many of the wood models have been converted to metal since production started in 1955. Mooney built just over 2,600 180-horsepower models until 1978. About 5,000 200-horsepower models were built from 1964 until 1998.

Mooney also offered a few surprises along the way, like the fixed-gear Master built from 1963 until 1965. (Most of these have been converted to retractable gear.) Along the way, they also offered bigger engines and longer fuselages and they even attempted a pressurized version called the Mustang. (A Mooney on steroids, only 32 were built.) But for reasonable cost and economical operation, the M20 line is the best model available.

Piper Arrow 180

In 1967, Piper took their reliable and easy-to-fly Cherokee 180 and retracted the wheels. The result was an aircraft that became a great trainer, an economical cross-country cruiser, and a transition aircraft for the masses of pilots who wanted to move up the Piper ladder. The cockpit layout is consistent with all other Cherokees with the exceptions of a constant-speed

Piper Arrow 180	
Cost of Operation	****
Cockpit Comfort	***
Cruise Speed	**
Useful Load	****
Serviceability and Parts Availability	***
Engine manufacturer and horsepower	Lycoming 180hp
Construction	Metal
Landing gear	Retractable
Maximum seating	4
Gross weight	2,500 lb
Useful load	1,120 lb
Cruise speed	141 mph
Stall speed	53 mph
Takeoff run	820 ft.
Takeoff run 50 feet	1,240 ft.
Landing roll	776 ft.
Standard fuel capacity	50 gal
Range	550 mi.
Fuel burn per hour	10 GPH
Last year of production	1971
Manufacturer in business?	Yes
Good availability?	No

propeller and retractable-gear lever: items that made the Arrow 180 a popular complex trainer.

The 180-horsepower model remained in production until 1971 with 1,156 built. Performance is in line with the other aircraft in its class. It's a better two-seat aircraft than a four-, and it can cruise at about 160 miles per hour on a good day. And if you are a Cherokee 140 pilot, the transition to retractable gear takes nothing more than a few hours of flying time with an instructor to perfect.

In 1969, Piper tried to eliminate gear-up landings by adding an automatic gear extension system comprising a pitot tube mounted on the side of the aircraft to respond to air speed and lower the gear without the pilot's help. As long as the system works it's a nice safety feature, but sometimes it gets plugged or wires are broken and it fails.

Piper Arrow 200

As is always with engineers, the need for speed infected Piper, and the result was an Arrow with a 200-horsepower Lycoming engine. The large engine enabled an increase in gross weight and bumped the cruise speed to about 161 miles per hour. Wait, that's the same as the 180-horsepower model! What really happened was that the bigger engine gave the Arrow better climb and useful load, but it didn't really help the cruise speed.

The 200-horsepower Arrow has been built from 1969 until the present. Airframe changes began in 1972 when the fuselage was lengthened five inches and the tail size was increased. In 1973, the cabin area was enlarged, giving passengers a little more comfort. The thick, short "Hershey bar" wing was changed to the tapered wing in 1977, and in 1978 a Turbo Arrow

continued on page 120

The 200-horsepower Piper Arrow has been produced from 1969 to the present. The bigger engine and retractable gear increase the cruise speed to 140 knots, while maintaining the same ease of handling typical of the smaller 180 and Archer.

In 1979, Piper modified the Arrow 200 to a T-tail and offered both turbo and normally aspirated models. The T-tail, however, had a reputation for being ineffective at low speeds and during takeoffs and landings. The design put the elevator out of the prop blast, reducing control. In 1990, Piper lowered the tail due to customer dissatisfaction.

The panel of both the Arrow 180 and 200 is identical to that in the Cherokee and Warrior models, with the exception of extra levers to operate the landing gear and constant-speed propeller.

Above: The Cherokee Six is Piper's six-place, fixed-gear; it was designed to compete with the Cessna 206. Produced from 1965 to 1979 before it was renamed the Saratoga, the Cherokee Six was originally offered with a 260-horsepower engine and then in 1966 with an optional 300-horsepower engine. *Photo courtesy of LeRoy Cook*

The Cherokee line has the same panel layout from the 140 to the light twins. Except for its size, this Cherokee 6 panel is almost identical to that in the Cherokee 140. *Photo courtesy of John B. McLaughlin*

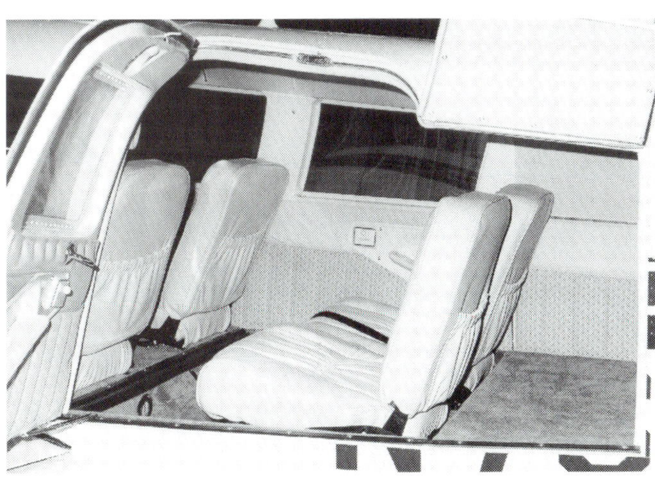

One advantage of the Cherokee Six is the large cargo/passenger door located on the rear left side of the aircraft. This allows passengers access to the rear of the plane without climbing over the wing and through the seats. *Photo courtesy of John B. McLaughlin*

Above: The Cherokee 235 was produced from 1964 to 1977. Basically an enlarged Cherokee 180 with a Lycoming 235-horsepower engine, the 235 was later replaced by the Dakota (1979 to 1994) and the Turbo Dakota (1979 only).

A fixed-pitch propeller came standard with the 235; a constant-speed propeller became one of the model's more popular options.

Like most of the Cherokee line, the 235 panel is basically the same as that found in the 140 and 180. Enough space was offered to allow a full compliment of avionics.

The only difference between the 235 panel and the Dakota panel shown here is the control for the latter's constant-speed propeller.

Below: In 1980, Piper converted the Cherokee Six to the fixed-gear Saratoga. *Photo courtesy of Norm Goyer*

Continued from page 115
was introduced with a Continental six-cylinder, 200-horsepower engine and turbocharger.

In 1979 Piper changed the Arrow's tail to a "T" configuration, a style that lasted until 1990 when Piper converted to a conventional tail. Most T-tail Arrows are cheaper to buy on the used market, but they require more runway and a little different technique to wrench maximum performance out of them. In recent years the Arrow has been built on demand only. With all the variations (turbo, T-tail, etc.) the Arrow 200 accounts for about 1,962 aircraft.

Piper Arrow 200	
Cost of Operation	*****
Cockpit Comfort	***
Cruise Speed	**
Useful Load	****
Serviceability and Parts Availability	*****
Engine manufacturer and horsepower	Lycoming 200hp
Construction	Metal
Landing gear	Retractable
Maximum seating	4
Gross weight	2,600 lb
Useful load	1,141 lb
Cruise speed	144 mph
Stall speed	56 mph
Takeoff run	770 ft.
Takeoff run 50 feet	1,600 ft.
Landing roll	780 ft.
Standard fuel capacity	50 gal
Range	600 mi.
Fuel burn per hour	10 GPH
Last year of production	2001
Manufacturer in business?	Yes
Good availability?	Yes

Piper Cherokee Six

The Piper Cherokee Six was introduced in 1965 as a long-nosed, fixed-gear cargo- and passenger-hauling aircraft. Its type certificate actually lists it as a seven-place aircraft, but the 1,453 260-horsepower examples produced from 1965 to 1978 would be slightly underpowered with that much of a load.

The Cherokee Six (PA32-260) was designed with a door on the right side and a large cargo door at the left rear. Because the 260 model is considered underpowered by freight haulers and heavy-load pilots, prices are typically lower than 300-horsepower versions. In reality the 260, if carefully loaded, can be just as good a buy as any of the higher priced 300s. Most of the aircraft are flown as four- to six-seat aircraft anyway, allowing passengers extra room for comfort and baggage. A baggage nose behind the engine and in front of the windshield not only keeps baggage out of the cabin, it also helps offset the long center of gravity caused by the length of the aircraft.

Piper Cherokee Six	
Cost of Operation	***
Cockpit Comfort	*****
Cruise Speed	***
Useful Load	**
Serviceability and Parts Availability	****
Engine manufacturer and horsepower	Lycoming 300hp
Construction	Metal
Landing gear	Tri-gear
Maximum seating	7
Gross weight	3,400 lb
Useful load	1,611 lb
Cruise speed	146 mph
Stall speed	55 mph
Takeoff run	1,050 ft.
Takeoff run 50 feet	1,500 ft.
Landing roll	630 ft.
Standard fuel capacity	50 gal
Optional fuel capacity	84 gal
Range	673 mi.
Fuel burn per hour	16 GPH
Last year of production	1979
Manufacturer in business?	Yes
Good availability?	Yes

For those who want a little more power, the PA28-300 introduced in 1966 with a 300-horsepower Lycoming is fuel injected rather than carbureted like the 260. Produced until 1979, more than 2,300 Cherokee Six 300s were built.

Piper Cherokee 235/Dakota

The Cherokee 235 (PA28-135) is Piper's answer to the Cessna 182. In 1964, Piper took a slightly enlarged Cherokee fuselage and added a 235-horsepower Lycoming engine. The aircraft was initially offered with a fixed-pitch propeller as standard, but had a constant-speed as an option.

The 235 seems to be just a plain old Cherokee with a big engine. Cruise is about 153 miles per hour (less than an Arrow but better than a Cherokee 180), and the 235 has a reputation for being able to haul just about anything the pilot can get in the doors on about 14 gallons per hour.

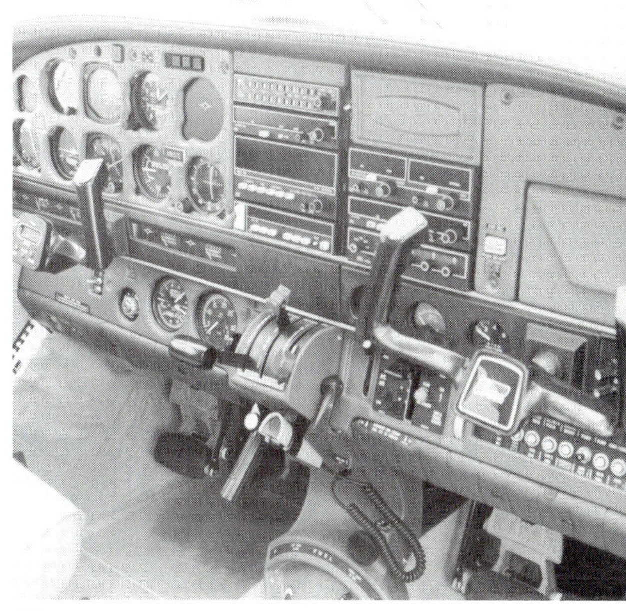

Both the Cherokee Six and the Saratoga have roomy cabins and instrument panels with plenty of room for avionics. *Photo courtesy of* Aero Trader

Piper Cherokee 235/Dakota	
Cost of Operation	***
Cockpit Comfort	****
Cruise Speed	*****
Useful Load	*****
Serviceability and Parts Availability	****
Engine manufacturer and horsepower	Lycoming 235hp
Construction	Metal
Landing gear	Tri-gear
Maximum seating	4
Gross weight	3,000 lb
Useful load	1,392 lb
Cruise speed	143 mph
Stall speed	56 mph
Takeoff run	886 ft.
Takeoff run 50 feet	1,216 ft.
Landing roll	825 ft.
Standard fuel capacity	72 gal
Range	650 mi.
Fuel burn per hour	12 GPH
Last year of production	1994
Manufacturer in business?	Yes
Good availability?	Yes

In 1973, Piper dubbed the aircraft the "Charger," and gave it a 5-inch fuselage stretch, a larger tail, and a 100-pound increase in the gross weight. In 1975, the model name was changed to the "Pathfinder," a handle that remained with the aircraft until 1977, when it was discontinued. During that time about 2,100 aircraft were built.

In 1979, the aircraft was re-introduced as the PA28-236 Dakota with the same 235-horsepower Lycoming engine and a new improved tapered wing that increased the cruise speed to 165 miles per hour. Although 750 Dakotas were manufactured until 1994, it appears only one was built in 1990 and none were built in 1991 and 1992.

While the Dakota and 235 are not fuel misers for their speed, they do afford a real four-place aircraft with fixed gear.

Piper Saratoga

The Saratoga replaced the Cherokee Six in 1980 and has been in production ever since in one form or another. The Saratoga maintains a long fuselage

Piper Saratoga	
Cost of Operation	***
Cockpit Comfort	*****
Cruise Speed	****
Useful Load	*
Serviceability and Parts Availability	****
Engine manufacturer and horsepower	Lycoming 300hp
Construction	Metal
Landing gear	Tri-gear
Maximum seating	7
Gross weight	3,600 lb
Useful load	1,660 lb
Cruise speed	150 mph
Stall speed	58 mph
Takeoff run	1,183 ft.
Takeoff run 50 Feet	1,759 ft.
Landing roll	732 ft.
Standard fuel capacity	102 gal
Range	745 mi.
Fuel burn per hour	16 GPH
Last year of production	1999
Manufacturer in business?	Yes
Good availability?	Yes

and the cargo door, but is offered with retractable landing gear and a turbocharger. In addition, the cabin is often laid out in a "club seating" (face-to-face) arrangement.

Cruise speeds range from 172 miles per hour for the fixed-gear version to 184 miles per hour for the turbo, retractable-gear models.

Piper Turbo Dakota

The Turbo Dakota is a misfit of sorts, designed around the Dakota airframe with a Continental 200-horsepower engine and a turbocharger. The Continental was initially noted for problems like overheating and cylinder cracking, but since 1979, the Turbo Dakota's only production year, after market intercoolers and better baffling have reduced or eliminated the problems.

The Turbo Dakota, because of its name, is often compared to the PA28-236 Dakota, but the Dakota has a much bigger engine and should more accurately be compared to the Archer or Arrow lines. When compared to those aircraft, the Turbo Dakota is a great performer. In fact, it's what I would call a "sleeper," offering 77-gallon fuel tanks, 177 miles per hour cruise, and four-seat capability. And with a turbocharger, mountain crossings and high altitudes are possible.

The Turbo Dakota's biggest drawback is probably its low production numbers.

Produced in 1979 only, the Turbo Dakota, along with the Dakota (1979 to 1994), replaced the Cherokee 235, which itself is a 180 with a 235-horsepower Lycoming engine.

The Turbo Dakota has the airframe and wing of the Archer with a 200-horsepower Continental six-cylinder engine. While its turbocharger offers respectable high-altitude performance, customers in 1979 by and large preferred the normally aspirated Dakota, ergo the Turbo Dakota's one-year production run.

Piper Turbo Dakota	
Cost of Operation	****
Cockpit Comfort	****
Cruise Speed	*****
Useful Load	*****
Serviceability and Parts Availability	***
Engine manufacturer and horsepower	Continental 200hp
Construction	Metal
Landing gear	Tri-gear
Maximum seating	4
Gross weight	2,900 lb
Useful load	1,321 lb
Cruise speed	154 mph
Stall speed	59 mph
Takeoff run	963 ft.
Takeoff run 50 feet	1,402 ft.
Landing roll	861 ft.
Standard fuel capacity	72 gal
Range	591 mi.
Fuel burn per hour	10 GPH
Last year of production	1979
Manufacturer in business?	Yes
Good availability?	No

If you are looking for an aircraft that offers cockpit comfort, two-door access, and unique looks, Rockwell's Commander 112 or 114 might meet your requirements. The Commander's trailing-link, retractable landing gear allow most pilots to impress their passengers with consistently smooth landings. Produced from 1972 to present by Commander Aircraft, the 112/114 line is often equated with luxury and high performance.

One noticeable trait of the Commander 112 and 114 is the "cruciform" tail. While unique in single-engine private aircraft, it's common on larger aircraft around the world. Usual debates about the design center on airflow and prop blast and how they affect elevator and rudder control.

Socata TB20 Trinidad

The Trinidad is the sports car of this category. Actually a fairly small aircraft, the TB20 is not much bigger than the Tampico and Tobago in the previous chapter, but is equipped with a 250-horsepower Lycoming engine and retractable gear. This combination, along with a slick appearance and fuselage, yields impressive cruise numbers—the Trinidad's book cruise is 188 miles per hour.

The type certificate for the Trinidad (as well as the Tobago) lists five seats, but with a rear seat designed to hold three, it can be a little cramped. This is a pretty modern-looking aircraft, with curved lines, an automotive-styled panel, and reclining bucket seats. As such, few are available on the used market. The TB20 has been produced from 1988 to the present, and the new models have been redesigned to give a smooth appearance and better performance numbers.

Rockwell Commander 112/114

The Commander 112 and 114 offer pilot and passengers great cockpit comfort at the expense of speed. The original 112 introduced in 1972 is powered by Continental's 200-horsepower engine. The 112 and 114 (unveiled in 1976) both have an appearance of size, inside and out. And that size transfers to cruise speed. The 112 can only bolster a book cruise speed of 155 miles per hour, if the pilot is lucky. The other unique characteristic of the Commanders is their "cruciform" tail design with the horizontal stabilizer and elevator mounted halfway up the vertical fin. While the design is supposed to assist in handling, its real advantage is purely aesthetic—the one thing Commanders do well is look good.

Of the two, the 114 is the better choice if you are looking for speed. Produced with a 260-horsepower engine, the 114 can attain cruise speeds up to 188 miles per hour if equipped with a turbocharger. But even if you didn't fly fast for the money, you'll ride in luxury; Commanders have always been known as roomy, high-performance singles. The 112 and 112TC (turbocharged) were produced from 1972 until 1979. The 114 and 114TC have been produced from 1976 to the present.

Rockwell Commander 112	
Cost of Operation	****
Cockpit Comfort	****
Cruise Speed	**
Useful Load	*
Serviceability and Parts Availability	***
Engine manufacturer and horsepower	Lycoming 200hp
Construction	Metal
Landing gear	Retractable
Maximum seating	4
Gross weight	2,550 lb
Useful load	1,020 lb
Cruise speed	143 mph
Stall speed	53 mph
Takeoff run	880 ft.
Takeoff run 50 feet	1,460 ft.
Landing roll	1,310 ft.
Standard fuel capacity	60 gal
Range	750 mi.
Fuel burn per hour	10 GPH
Last year of production	1977
Manufacturer in business?	Yes
Good availability?	No

Rockwell Commander 114	
Cost of Operation	***
Cockpit Comfort	****
Cruise Speed	*****
Useful Load	****
Serviceability and Parts Availability	*****
Engine manufacturer and horsepower	Lycoming 260hp
Construction	Metal
Landing gear	Retractable
Maximum seating	4
Gross weight	3,140 lb
Useful load	1,235 lb
Cruise speed	157 mph
Stall speed	55 mph
Takeoff run	1,400 ft.
Takeoff run 50 feet	1,990 ft.
Landing roll	750 ft.
Standard fuel capacity	68 gal
Range	665 mi.
Fuel burn per hour	14 GPH
Last year of production	2001
Manufacturer in business?	Yes
Good availability?	Yes

Socata TB-20 Trinidad	
Cost of Operation	****
Cockpit Comfort	****
Cruise Speed	*****
Useful Load	*
Serviceability and Parts Availability	****
Engine manufacturer and horsepower	Lycoming 250hp
Construction	Metal
Landing gear	Retractable
Maximum seating	5
Gross weight	3,083 lb
Useful load	1,339 lb
Cruise speed	167 mph
Stall speed	54 mph
Takeoff run	1,193 ft.
Takeoff run 50 feet	1,954 ft.
Landing roll	755 ft.
Standard fuel capacity	86 gal
Range	1,100 mi.
Fuel burn per hour	14 GPH
Last year of production	2001
Manufacturer in business?	Yes
Good availability?	No

The Socata TB20 is a retractable gear enhancement of the TB9. The TB20 offers a 250-horsepower, six-cylinder Lycoming engine with a cruise speed of 164 knots. The TB21 TC is a turbocharged version of the TB20 with a cruise speed of 187 knots. *Photo courtesy of Norm Goyer*

References

Aero Trader
P.O. Box 2576
Norfolk, VA 23501
800-407-2335
www.aerotrader.com

Aircraft Blue Book Price Digest
P.O. Box 12901
Overland Park, KS 66282
800-654-6776
www.aircraftbluebook.com

Aircraft Owners and Pilots Association
421 Aviation Way
Frederick, MD 21701
800-872-2672
www.aopa.com

Aircraft Value Reference
P.O. Box 23321
Shawnee Mission, KS 66283
800-773-8733
www.vrefpub.com

Cessna Aircraft Company
P.O. Box 7706
Wichita, KS 67277
316-517-6000
www.cessna.com

Des Moines Flying Service, Inc.
P.O. Box 35126
Des Moines, IA 50315
515-256-5300
www.dmfs.com

Diamond Aircraft
1560 Crumlin Sideroad
London, ON, Canada N5V 1S2
519-457-4000
www.diamondair.com

Experimental Aircraft Association
P.O. Box 3086
Oshkosh, WI 54903
800-843-3612
www.eaa.org

Exec 1 Aviation
3737 Convenience Rd.
Ankeny, IA 50021
515-965-1020
www.exec1aviation.com

Hap's Air Service
2508 Airport Dr.
Ames, IA 50010
515-232-4310

Socata Aircraft, Inc.
7501 Pembroke Rd.
Pembroke Pines, FL 33023
954-893-1400
www.socataaircraft.com

Trade-A-Plane
P.O. Box 509
Crossville, TN 38557
800-337-5263
www.tradeaplane.com

Index

Other MBI Publishing Company titles of interest:

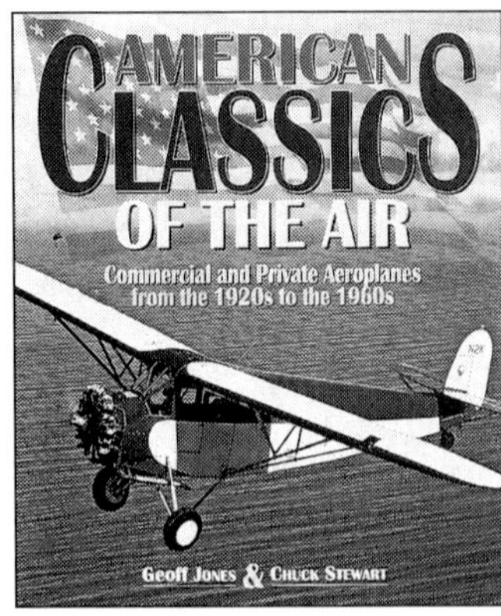

American Classics of the Air
ISBN: 0-7603-0901-9

Cessan Citation Jets
ISBN: 0-7603-0785-7

Executive Jets
ISBN: 0-7603-0558-7

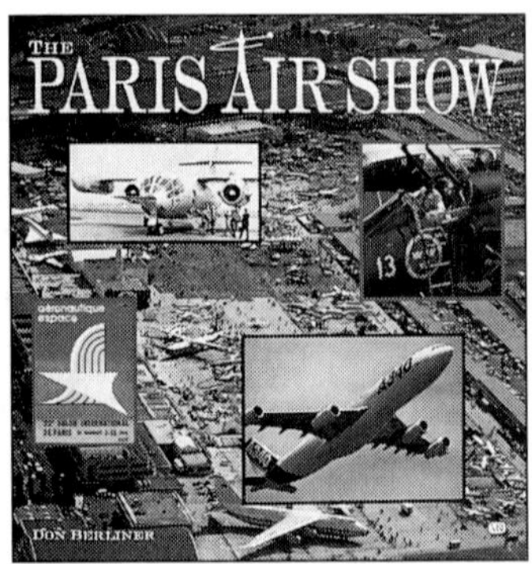

Paris Air Show
ISBN: 0-7603-0728-8

Race with the Wind: How Air Racing Advanced Aviation
ISBN: 0-7603-0729-6

Wings of Yesteryear: The Golden Age of Private Aircraft
ISBN: 0-7603-0397-5

Find us on the internet at www.motorbooks.com 1-800-826-6600